AF575267

DOLGE

DOLGE

by ELEANOR FRANZ

HERKIMER COUNTY HISTORICAL SOCIETY

This book about the life and work of Alfred Dolge conforms to the stated objectives of the Herkimer County Historical Society—the discovery, collection, and publication of history relating to the part of New York State first known as Tyron, and later Herkimer County. It represents the culmination of many years of research, and the author's generosity in sharing her work with the society exemplifies the local historian's dedication and skill in research. The society is indebted to the Publishing Center for Cultural Resources for assistance.

S. M. Alvis, Chairman
The Publications Committee
Herkimer County Historical Society

Library of Congress Cataloging in Publication Data

Franz, Eleanor.
Dolge.

Includes index.
1. Dolge, Alfred, 1848–1922 2. Piano makers—United States—Biography.
ML424.D64F7 786.2'1'0924 [B] 80-12117
ISBN 0-89062-075-X

Produced by Publishing Center for Cultural Resources,
New York City

Designed by Sara Seagull

Manufactured in the United States of America

TABLE OF CONTENTS

For Lorenz

FOREWORD

No more unlikely area for an 1870's experiment in social welfare could be imagined than Brockett's Bridge, New York, where three hundred men, women, and children lived on small subsistence farms and raised hops or milk cows, worked in the bark woods or on the Erie Canal, shot deer, butchered pigs, and tapped maple trees for a livelihood. To this town, set in its lovely forest valley, came Alfred Dolge. Yellowed newspapers, so weak at the seams that one must handle them like cobwebs, describe a career that reads like a novel. One of thousands of young men who came as immigrants to America, he came already possessed by an idea. Steeped in the Social Democratic teachings of forward looking men in his native Germany, and with the brains to make his ideals into a force propelling others, he dreamed of wealth in this new country—not simply for himself, but for the men who worked beside him. He had an idea that in this new world it would be possible to manufacture things that were both finer and less costly by encouraging free labor than was possible using the half-slave labor of the old apprentice shops of Europe. He proved it in the making of piano felt better than that made in Europe, and then—not stopping there—in the making of all the parts of the piano. But piano making was only a means to the end he had in view.

It is natural for those of an established order to distrust those who wish change; that a man who wished to change conditions was to be found in the class of emerging industrialists was profoundly disturbing. Those who were already prosperous looked at him askance, and those who had not his vision whispered behind his back. But Dolge is remembered, and deserves to be better known, for his foresight. His evaluation of the needs of workers was far in advance of the thinking that would lead eventually to what we now speak of as Social Security.

The drama of Alfred Dolge's life is an absorbing one. As one of those who came in contact with it, I have long felt a compulsion to share it. This book is the result. —E.F.

CHAPTER 1

THE NEWCOMER

Take any picture of an upstate New York village in the 1870s, color it with golden glow, shade it with elms and frame it with woods and water, and you have Brockett's Bridge. The houses were two-storied and square, sturdy but not large. Some had one-story kitchens attached at the side, and all had inset porches with square pillars—an architecture similar to the New England homes from which many of the residents came. It was less pretentious but equally pure in line. A covered bridge, which had given the place its name, crossed a wildly rushing river that further downstream descended in a series of waterfalls. From underneath the bridge there usually hung two or three large rugs, dangling from ropes into rushing water. Spruce water was good for wool. The water was clear but had a peculiar tint of brownish green. A long two-story building by the stream was the old tannery, now deserted. Mouldering piles of spruce bark lay across the way, next to the empty boarding house where the tannery workers had lived.

The stream that wound its way through the little settlement had been known to the Indians as the Tegahuhharoghwe or Auskerada, the stream of many fishes. Very few Indians had ventured this far north of the Mohawk Valley, however. It was too cold. The Favilles and the Spencers had come pushing and pulling their worldly goods in oxcarts and covered wagons soon after the end of the Revolutionary War. But this was no crossroads town; there were no roads that crossed. The old Military Road, running northward from Saratoga to Sackett's Harbor, plunged down Brockett's Hill and over the covered bridge, then pushed its way up past the cemetery to Salisbury and Diamond Hill. Scattered along this dusty thoroughfare were a tavern and a few pillared old houses; by the stream were mills for sawing and grinding. The hundreds of teams and the thousands of cattle passing through from Albany to Sackett's Harbor before the Canal opened had been the town's greatest excitement. From the tavern porch Clinton Brockett had read the news of

Lincoln's death; the old soldiers had come down out of the hills to hear it.[1]

During the Civil War there had been a free church that was a station on the Underground Railroad. Reuben Faville put most of the money in it, so after the war they deeded it to him. Finally it would become the Barney Opera House. Altogether there had been three churches. There was a small school, set beyond a walk that passed under two rows of elms. Along with the empty boarding house, a blacksmith's shop, a post office shared by Zephi and Clinton Brockett—alternating as Democrat and Republican—a few farmhouses dozed pleasantly beside the river. There was a carpenter shop, and there was Spofford's tin shop where roofing, teakettles, and sap buckets were turned out, to be peddled by Mr. Spofford from a cart. A cheese box factory, and a small venture in carpet weaving both struggled along for a time. The industries here had all been crafts except for the tannery. Isaac Heller made barrels in a cooperage on the road to Little Falls, eight miles away. The priest at Salisbury had given orders for many barrels to ship pork to Ireland during the famine there. The cheese factory had five or six men. Cheese tubs, some as large as eight feet across, red outside and white inside, and milk pans three or four feet high spoke of the predominance of cheese making, a skill brought from England. Small cheese factories and hop houses dotted the village. T. P. Green ran a general store, as did Addision Lamberson, and David Loucks had a cobbler's shop.[2]

In the days of the tannery, teamsters who leased horses got three dollars a day in the back woods; if their loads were heavy, they hitched on another team. Before the war, Major D.B. Winton had built a Georgian mansion that Charlie Cramer's grandfather, a carpenter, worked on for two years. It had hand-carved moldings and banisters of curly maple. A picket fence ran around it, and in the back was a double woodshed where they backed the teams to throw off a load of wood. It was the grandest house in the village when built in 1839.

The last run of leather in the tannery had been in 1871; after that, Brockett's Bridge had fallen into the doldrums.[3] Its population remained stationary at about three hundred souls and might have dwindled away to nothing had it not been for a newcomer whose tremendous energy was to change it all.

For a traveler approaching from the virgin forest and silent lakes of the north, the land fell away from the dirt road into a little valley encircled with evergreens. From the darker indentation that marked the course of the river, the hills rose steeply, and behind were the mountains, blue and clear against a gold and purple sunset. As the shadows lengthened, bringing the coolness of the night air, the mountains appeared close and distinct. Dotting the valley, in clearings for farmland, were small, drab, unpainted houses, as many as twenty clustered together.

This was the borderline of the wilderness. Here the Adirondacks began and from here they spread, a solid cover, from the North Country into Canada. Behind the traveler was nothing but one or two smaller settlements, a few local sawmills, French Canadians, trappers, deer, and bears.

Joe Helterline, who owned a sawmill in the north woods, drove the newcomer to Brockett's Bridge on April 11, 1874, when the waters of the Tegahuhharoghwe were free of ice.[4] Joe was of German descent himself, and recognized this fellow by his accent as a recent arrival from Deutschland. He wore the clothes of a city man, now somewhat dusty from a long trip. By any standard he was good looking, with broad shoulders, a high forehead, dark curly hair, fine dark eyes, and ruddy coloring. When he spoke, white teeth flashed, and he conveyed a feeling of vitality so overpowering that it invested the person with whom he talked with a sense of well being.

Joe knew this passenger's name was Alfred Dolge and that he came from New York, where he was a felt manufacturer and importer of piano parts. He had often traveled through the Adirondacks to buy lumber for piano sounding boards. The two men had just come from Joe's own sawmill, up in the Oregon section of the Adirondacks, and were on their way to Little Falls. But Brockett's Bridge had aroused the interest of the stranger. In New York, he said, he had met a General J. P. Spofford, who had told him it was a likely spot for felt making. Joe now volunteered, since he liked what he saw of the newcomer, that the old tannery buildings were for sale cheap. "Stop the horse," Alfred Dolge said. He looked long and hard at the wooden buildings by the stream, at the rushing water with its promise of power.

Later, Alfred Dolge would say that it was as though he had looked upon his native Saxony, left behind six years before. A belief that he had found the place for his felt-making venture had taken root in his mind.

As long ago as 1755 the rich bottom lands in Manheim, south of Brockett's Bridge, had been settled by Palatine Germans—formerly wealthy farmers who had been driven from the Palatinate by taxation and persecution. Between 1800 and 1900 the German-speaking population of Europe had increased from 20 million to more than 60 million. As the working and living conditions of a growing industrial population worsened, the migration from Germany to America had risen steadily; in the years from 1871 to 1880, the average annual total came to 62,500.[5] Alfred Dolge had been in the vanguard of that migration.

Born in Chemnitz, Saxony in 1848, he had been six months old when his father, Christian August Dolge, went to prison under a death sentence for having taken part in the short-lived revolution of 1848.[6] He was eventually pardoned and released; in the meantime, Alfred and his two older brothers had been supported by their mother, Auguste von Steitz Dolge, a determined woman who opened a dry goods business.

Under her guidance, Alfred's commercial instincts showed themselves early. As he recalled later, "During the Christmas holiday season, I had to assist in my mother's business selling dry goods. My work consisted chiefly in doing errands and getting from the wholesalers such goods as might be wanted immediately. I was then between nine and ten years of age. In one of the wholesale houses I found a big lot of printed petticoats of a very pleasing design. They took my fancy to such an extent that I took a dozen of them along to show to mother as a good Christmas article. Mother was not at all of my opinion." Nevertheless, he sold them all—"at a very large profit"—within two days.[7]

He took equal pride in recalling how, by going through the wastebaskets of the leading merchants and booksellers in Leipzig, he collected a stock of postage stamps, and thus capitalized on the craze among his contemporaries for stamp collecting. To give his young customers an equal chance at some of the choicer ones, it occurred to Alfred that he might run a lottery. Even at a quarter of a pfennig apiece, his stamp lotteries became so popular that he soon had thirty German dollars on his books, an enormous amount of money. His teachers warned him and then clamped down. They not only confiscated his stock in trade, but even deprived him of school honors.

Thus, at the age of nine, he recalled with a shrug, "ended my career as a dealer in postage stamps."

When Christian Dolge was finally pardoned and released from prison, he imposed drillmaster standards upon his boys. Alfred's days in public school ended when he was thirteen. He now had to go into his father's trade as a piano maker. Although he liked business much better, his father insisted that he must learn a trade. His Uncle Louis, of whom Alfred was fond, was his foreman. "Learn to like your craft, boy," he urged him softly. Not content with the apprenticeship, however, both his uncle and mother gently propelled Alfred through the evening high school maintained by the Masonic Lodge of Leipzig. For the rest of his life, the diploma he earned would be displayed in a frame on his bedroom wall; a love of scholarship had been born in him.

Neither apprenticeship nor evening school engaged all of his faculties, though. At the age of fourteen he organized a club for young men with the earnest aim of "keeping them away from temptations." This was to be accomplished by making the club's meetings "more attractive than the saloon or dance hall." To this end the youthful reformer provided, as he later wrote, "all sorts of inexpensive entertainments and at least twice a month I induced some prominent man to give us a lecture on the topics of the day."

That was not enough. After two years as president, Alfred discovered that he could not overcome his members' insistence that girls be allowed to join. He gave in finally and made arrangements with a dancing master to take over the club once a week with instructions for members of both sexes. He glowered at first, but not after a slender dark girl appeared. Her name was Augusta Anna Horn. She was a year younger than Alfred. As he later recalled, "I was the only one of the entire club who came out of it with a serious love affair. She became my wife."

The sober gatherings of the club continued, and one of the men whom Alfred persuaded to address the membership was Wilhelm Liebknecht, a friend of his father's who had been exiled to England for his part in the revolution of 1848. After Liebknecht returned to Leipzig in 1862, the friendship had been resumed. During these years Liebknecht was formulating the ideas that were to become the basis of the Social Democratic party, of which he became the founder of 1875. As an intimate friend of Christian Dolge, he directed Alfred's reading for two years. For two or three evenings a week Alfred studied with him, and through the writings of Adam Smith, an advocate of free trade and unlimited competitive enterprise, as well as David Ricardo and John Stuart Mill, began his first real study of social problems.

Thus, out of thought and discussion fostered by the reading matter that was strewn about the house and by the example of a father who had not been afraid to suffer for his own political principles, an eager young mind was being formed. In later years, the ideas of his own chief mentor, Liebknecht, were to become a great force in persuading Bismarck to enact social legislation that "anticipated by several decades similar enactments in England and France, to say nothing of the more laggard labor policy of the United States."[8] By then, Dolge himself would have embarked on an effort to put his own ideas into effect. In the meantime, German liberals saw the United States as the country of progress. So on July 6, 1866, at the age of seventeen Alfred Dolge left for America aboard a sailing vessel, the *Victoria.*

His apprenticeship having come to an end, as he wrote later, "I was desirous of following the custom of the average German to go out into the world."[9]

"The Austro-Prussian war having just broken out and [with] business paralyzed all over Europe, I concluded to go to America, to which plan, however, my father, as well as my mother were opposed and would therefore not aid me. Having no means of any kind I had to borrow the necessary money to pay my passage to America from kindly disposed relatives and friends."[10]

He traveled in steerage, where the trip was a nightmare. Though printed contracts guaranteeing rations had been issued to the passengers, they were forgotten once the open sea was reached. Half of the passengers died during the sixty-three-day voyage. "We left Hamburg with 336 passengers on board," Dolge later wrote, "and arrived in New York numbering only 132 [on September 9, 1866]." It became a kind of rule that when a passenger died, whatever had been near him in a bunk had to go overboard. Four men who died had slept in the same bunk with Alfred, and most of his clothes followed them into the waves.

The widow of a man who died of ship colic engaged his sympathy. She had eight children (the smallest a six-month-old baby) and was close to starving. Having found a way into the captain's larder, Alfred helped himself to some biscuits and regularly brought them to the mother. Thanks to a little money when he left Hamburg, he had been able to buy food from the cook, and he was able to earn enough by peeling potatoes and washing dishes to keep himself alive. But now he went to the captain with his contract and a demand for the promised rations, threatening him with exposure if they were not produced.

The captain threatened in his turn to lock up the young upstart, and after a "miserable whelp" reported his theft of biscuits, the threat was carried out. A few days later the boy was free again, unrepentant and taking note of everything around him. The captain had a girl who "roomed with him," as Alfred delicately put it. On fine days the "contemptible vulgar brute" engaged a sailor to play the accordion so that he might dance on deck. Passengers were permitted to watch. The rear of the ship was deserted, and on one of the dancing days, Alfred opened the slats of the chicken coop. A hundred fowls that had been destined for the captain's own table went overboard instead, and this time the culprit was undetected.

By the end of the voyage, besides having his sympathies engaged, he had his eyes opened to the weaknesses of ordinary human beings. With typical thoroughness he had prepared a statement for the German consul of what the passengers had suffered, but when Alfred tried to get their signatures, all but three of them refused. As they neared Staten Island, the captain gave the survivors fresh pork from three hogs he had had killed—so that, at last full of pork and peas and within sight of green land, they forgot their troubles. Alfred looked at them with disillusionment. He had been sure all would share his outrage.

He was landing at Castle Garden with twenty-five cents in his pocket—a common experience for German immigrants. Alfred spent his first night making "an immediate acquaintaince with the thousands of rats which had their circus every night in the old building."[11] Like Ben Franklin arriving in Philadelphia, Alfred spent his last pennies for milk and bread, setting out up Broadway to make his fortune. He could neither speak nor understand English. But the well-dressed people, the hurrying hither and thither, the whole air of New York inspired him. He found first a boarding house where German was spoken, and then a job in a piano factory.

The job evaporated after four months when the firm failed. For some months he worked at anything he could find. Once, having responded to a "Help Wanted" ad for a man to load coal at a dollar a day, he was beaten as a strikebreaker. He had no idea what he had done. This, he wrote, "was my first experience with unionism."[12] But he had observed the low wages in Germany, and had seen poverty and despair of men laid off because of illness or old age with nothing but their own meager savings.

Alfred's next venture took him to the farmlands of Wisconsin, lured by a scheme involving government land which came to nothing. He returned to New York with four dollars in his pocket. The four months he had spent in the West were interesting to Alfred largely because he found himself working on a farm near the house in which the great German liberal Carl Schurz, a friend of his father's, had lived. Schurz, long a hero to Alfred, had escaped being sentenced to death for his part in the revolution of 1848 by emigrating to America, where he helped the cause of the American negro, took part in the Civil War, and eventually became Secretary of the Interior under President Rutherford B. Hayes.

In 1868 Alfred gave in to the pleas of his father and mother and returned to Germany. To earn his way back, he later recalled, "I served as a stoker on the S.S. *Rhein*, which gave me an excellent opportunity to study mankind." It was also the only way he could get passage on a steamship, rather than one of the old sailing vessels. The contrast between the first-class passengers and the men who spent their lives feeding boilers in the hold of the ship was, he observed, "excellent food for reflection."

Three months in Germany persuaded him that a place in the family piano business was not for him. As he saw it, the old liberal spirit for which his father had fought in 1848 was doomed and the seeds of Prussian militarism, out of which would come a Kaiser Wilhelm and then a Hitler, were taking root. To Alfred the Prussian influence was depressingly rigid, materialistic, and prosaic. "Two and a half years' stay in America had utterly unfitted me to be content in the contracted narrow-minded atmosphere of the business life of Germany," he later wrote.[13]

He saw no alternative but to return to America and work again in a factory. This time he found a place in New Haven, Connecticut at a piano factory where he had worked before—but this time at higher wages. Aware that he was really on his own now, he worked very hard at the bench, studied at night, and resolved to try his hand as an importer of piano materials—deerskins, steel wire, and so on.

He had not forgotten Anna Horn, the pretty dark girl at the dancing school in Leipzig. Now that he had settled on making a career in America, and was earning enough to support her, he did not intend to let her go out of his life. On December 22, 1868, his own twentieth birthday, Anna arrived in New York. They were married that same day and went by the night boat to New Haven. Alfred reported to the factory the next morning as usual, leaving poor little Anna all alone. But she had a strong character, and not once was there any hint that she complained of her lot. The love affair that began at the dancing school was to last a lifetime.

Not so the job in New Haven. There was a strike the following June, of which he did not approve. Nevertheless, Alfred's wages were cut along with those of the other men. Meanwhile, his experiment as an importer had continued. When the deerskins he had ordered from Germany arrived, he went to New York, carrying his bundles of skins, and tried selling them door to door. The gamble succeeded, and he ordered more skins.

His next venture was to try importing piano wire.

Frederick Malthusek, his employer, who was continually trying out new ideas in piano making, had begun to manufacture upright pianos, at a time when square pianos were still in vogue. Alfred believed that the wire he had been using was low in tension, and he told Malthusek so. He had a little of Poehlmann's wire, which Steinway and Knabe used in their pianos. Malthusek agreed to try it, and liked it. Now that Alfred had a market for the two products, he was ready to try his hand at a business of his own.

On July 6, 1869, he opened a store on Amity Street in New York City. A year later he moved to 122 East 13th Street, an address he was to maintain for twenty-seven years as an importer of piano materials.[14] By 1870 he had begun the great venture of his career, the manufacture of piano felt. In all of Europe, just three factories made that felt—one in Germany, one in France, and one in England. "Every one of those factories had their representatives in New York," Dolge later wrote, "and they refused to sell to me. Since felt was one of the most important articles in my line of business I had no choice but to manufacture the same." For one with his temperament, a difficulty was a challenge.

He started at Danbury, Connecticut, working in collaboration with a large manufacturer of hats. The expert felt makers who had been brought from Germany and France were unhappy in Connecticut and threatened to go back home unless the factory moved to New York. The felt they made was so good that Dolge planned to show it in competition with European felts at the 1873 World's Fair in Vienna. Meanwhile, with three friends, Dolge set up a small factory in a loft in Brooklyn, beginning with a single bale of wool. The felt was good, but his partners withdrew when payments for the felt-making machines fell due.[15] Shouldering the entire cost, Dolge continued to produce the felt, taking a loss which he was able to carry thanks to the profit he was making on the imported wire and leather. Sure that he had a good product, he took the gamble of traveling to Vienna to show it. Made with the hair of coney rabbits, its was firm and even all the way through. It took first prize.

"No one ever made felt as they did," one of the workers would say fifty years later. His name was Paul Franz. His hands in the expressive European way would show how Dolge had smoothed and worked the felt all through the night after finding it under a leaky roof at the Vienna Exposition. It dried evenly, so that it slit cleanly under a sharp blade as the judges looked on.

Orders for the felt came in, as Dolge had hoped they would. The next step was to look for better manufacturing facilities. And so it was, on that day in April 1874, that he had come to Brockett's Bridge. As he remembered afterward, "Both the country and the people reminded me so much of the Fatherland that I concluded to give myself wholly and unreservedly to the further development of this beautiful spot."[16]

That first time, Dolge stayed in Brockett's Bridge just long enough to make the acquaintance of the leading families: the Favilles, who were musical; the Brocketts, good farmers, who had been strong Abolitionists during the Civil War; and the Spoffords, relatives of the Civil War General J. P. Spofford, whom Dolge had known in New York. With the name of the owners of the tannery site in his pocket, he set off again for New York. Ten days later the transaction with them was completed, at a price of $7,000, to be paid off in installments of $1,000.[17]

Alfred's lovely dark-haired Anna waited in New York. On December 1, 1869 they had had their first son Rudolf in an apartment above the importing shop. With what interest she must have greeted his report on the new location.

Dolge was exultant about the move. The water power, the vacant buildings,[18] and the beautiful setting all pleased him tremendously. And something else, as yet no more than an unspoken thought, waited at the back of his mind to reveal itself as part of this venture—the opportunity for improving the condition of the working man.

CHAPTER 2

THE FACTORIES

The tannery had been closed for three years. Now, in 1874, industry came again to Brockett's Bridge—heavy machinery for felt making and ten skilled workmen from New York City.

Dolge made immediate use of the old tannery buildings for housing the machinery. The pure water that came from the Canada Lakes, twelve miles to the north, and descended in a series of falls to the Mohawk River, six miles farther south, made the location ideal. That water, which the women of the village had found so useful for washing their wool rugs, would be excellent for felt making, and the falls would be harnessed for energy.

The entrenched inhabitants, stern, hard-working pioneer New Englanders, tended to look with disfavor on innovation. As one put it, "Our idea of Germans was that they were as near wild Indians as could be imagined."[1]

Imagine two thousand wild Indians! That many, altogether, were to arrive in the village between 1874 and 1895. Some had heard of Dolge and been recruited in Germany. Many had been fresh off the boats when they were approached by his agents in New York. Some of the most skilled had worked for him in Brooklyn. To begin with, the felt was made by ten of them whom he had persuaded to give up their jobs in New York. For a while it seemed as though they had to live on crackers and cheese. There was no beer, only a little cider at meals, and "old cow" for meat. Maple sugar and syrup were in abundance; so were flapjacks and Indian meal, but these were not part of the normal German diet, nor was that New England staple, pork and beans. The sausages, the black bread, küchen, and sauerbraten of their native land were missing, and in retrospect those things seemed heavenly. It was said of the newcomers that "no one liked them, and they liked no one."

Brockett's Bridge was clearly not the El Dorado they had envisioned. The natives' habits were strange. A German worker wrote later,

"One thing was positive, I saw more chewing going on in the streets than I ever observed in New York. Why, even children were seen who kept their jaws moving constantly, as well as some of the fine young ladies. Horrified . . . I asked for an explanation and learned they were chewing gum and not tobacco." There were, the same man went on, "no sidewalks, a terrible hill that broke my front axletree—but the felt artists and the inhabitants were on a more friedly footing."[2]

Some of the men threatened to go back to New York. Some Dolge sent back himself, for he would not tolerate sloppy workmen. In his own words, "the unkempt and unwashed, careless pants-in-his-boots disappeared from our streets." Labor troubles were minor, since he always paid high wages and "from every quarter of the globe applicants for work arrived."[3]

At the beginning, Dolge divided his time between the factory and his importing business in New York. Twice a week he would leave New York at 9:00 P.M. by train, reaching Little Falls at about 4:00 in the morning. From there he walked the eight miles to Brockett's Bridge, since hiring a private team cost too much. Neither the dust of the sunbaked summer roads nor the snowdrifts of winter, which were often higher than his head, could stop him. The felt making had started as a convenience. It was to become an enthusiasm, an obsession, a necessity, and finally a nightmare. But having set a goal for himself, he "considered no sacrifice too great."[4] If he had to he would conquer everything in piano making but the elephants of Africa for the keys.

Diversity was in his mind from the start. By 1875 the manufacture of piano sounding boards had already begun. Dolge himself had learned how to glue and plane them during his apprenticeship in Europe. Lumber became a necessity. Before the end of 1875, a lumber yard was in operation on what came to be known as Dolge Avenue. Wheeler Knapp, a long-established lumber dealer outside the nearby town of Stratford, was another source of supply.

The factories were taking form. Dolge envisioned a picture of the completed buildings hanging in the office of every piano manufacturer in the country. Adhering to the shape of the former tannery, they were to be of native limestone, quarried at nearby Ingham's Mills; they would have supports reminiscent of the flying buttresses of Europe. James M. Gow and David Habich were to be in charge of a crew of Scottish stone masons, with some German workers assisting. The largest of the buildings would have four stories, with 300 by 70 feet of floor space. The first floor would contain the machinery for washing, fulling and hardening the wool. On the second was the carding room; when the wool left the cards, it was described as being like a spider's web. Next it was placed on a "former" and carried by elevator to the fulling room. On the third floor the finishing touches were put on the felts and piano hammers. The fourth floor was used for storage.[5]

Year by year, additions would be made. At first the factory ran entirely on water power. But when Dolge heard, in 1879, that Edison had perfected the electric dynamo, his imagination caught fire. The very first dynamo, in Brooklyn, was powered by steam. The second, installed by Dolge in his stone factory would become the first dynamo to be connected to a water wheel. By 1881 he would have added two stone boiler houses with large brick chimneys and an iron bridge connecting the main factory with the lumber yard on Dolge Avenue. From 1882 onward, the growth of the industries Dolge had launched would be phenomenal. All the buildings were to be equipped with automatic sprinklers and lighted by Edison's incandescent lamps.[6]

Long before then, Dolge would have refined the felt making process to a precise mathematical formula. In 1876 his product won first prize at the Philadelphia Centennial Exhibition. In 1877 he patented a hammer-covering machine, which exerted the necessary pressure for gluing the felt to the wood of the hammers.[7] That same year, a young Dane named Julius Breckwoldt, whom Dolge remembered from New York and persuaded to come to Brockett's Bridge, was put in charge of the lumber department. He had a quick mind and was good at bookkeeping. With his knack for figuring costs exactly down to the last cent was combined a tremendous physical endurance. He was a find—one of the many capable men whom Dolge was able to attract.

The son of a sea captain, Julius Breckwoldt had been born in Schleswig-Holstein. As a boy, living in a little house set in the midst of a garden shaded by pear trees, he lived on cheese, fish, and black bread and dreamed of adventure. During the American Civil War, his father had sailed a ship for the Union side and lost his life as a consequence. Seeing no future in Europe, Julius had emigrated to escape compulsory military training. In New York, where he had a job making piano moldings, he had discovered that city life did not suit him. He had made up his mind to go to Mexico and had begun studying Spanish when Alfred Dolge discovered him. With his ability to do his own timber cruising and to attend to the details of making sounding boards, moldings, and cases, by 1879 he had expanded the lumber department into a separate industry.[8]

By now the main factory was producing felt of many thicknesses—

some of it for organs, some for pianos, including the beautiful hammer felt that was used in the Steinway grand. But the absence of a tariff on the cheaper felt from Europe was causing Dolge to sell his at a loss. Possibly remembering the petticoats of his first business venture, he began looking about for ways to diversify and for new ideas for marketing the felt.

Among the men whom Dolge had brought from New York to Dolgeville was a felt maker named Ludwig Englehardt. With some scraps of felt he had made himself a pair of shoes, punching out the soles with hand dies. It happened that Daniel and William Green, sons of T. P. Green, who ran the general store in Brockett's Bridge, saw and were intrigued by Englehardt's experiment, since they were both shoe salesmen—Daniel for a firm in New York and William for one in Utica. Whether they or Dolge had the idea first is hard to determine; at any rate, Daniel asked for a dozen pairs as a sample, thinking they might make a nice little sideline.

Without hesitating a moment, Dolge agreed and immediately set aside a space in the felt mill for Englehardt. Only three men worked there at first; but six hundred pairs of shoes were sold in the first year, and after Daniel Green returned with a duplicate order, Dolge set about turning his piano felt makers into shoemakers. Thus, in 1881, the first felt shoe and slipper factory in America was born.[9] The soles and uppers were made of pure wool and sewn with waxed thread. "The advantages of wool in the manufacture of shoes," as a newspaper story a few years later observed, "are a particular power of absorption and transmission. It is a nonconductor of heat by which the feet are kept in an even temperature. It is not too much to say therefore, that Alfred Dolge, by developing the felt shoe industry became in large measure, a public benefactor."[10] The Hudson's Bay Company during the rush of prospectors to the Klondike region became one of Dolge's big accounts.[11]

As the lumber business expanded, Dolge began acquiring timberland as a source of supply. The Little Falls *Journal and Courier* reported in 1876 that he had purchased 18,000 acres in the Adirondacks and had built sawmills at Otter Lake and Port Leyden. In 1881, sawmills went up at Katawaba and Leipzig—the latter named in honor of Dolge's own home town.

Silas Kimm recalled the day Leipzig was christened. A truck loaded with kegs of lager drawn by a big prancing team was a part of the cavalcade of visitors to the village one hot Sunday in August. In an open air amphitheater was a band, and the crowd sang German songs and listened to German oratory. "To the clinking of beer steins the village was named 'Leipzig.' Many were the toasts."

It was in that year, 1881, on December 13 that another naming took place—a sign of how the town was growing and changing and of the gratitude its residents had come to feel toward the energetic young man who had made things happen. A petition was put in circulation by pairs of volunteers who went through the town and to the neighboring farms. People signed gladly, and as a result the name Brockett's Bridge was no more. From now on it would be known officially as Dolgeville.[12]

Under its new name, Dolgeville went on growing. In 1874 the population of Brockett's Bridge had been about three hundred, and its total wealth, according to the assessment rolls, was $30,000. By 1895 the population would have risen to 3,000 and the taxable property would be assessed at $1,200,000.

The year 1886 was the best to date. A new iron suspension bridge was built. The felt shoes and slippers had done so well that within two years they had outgrown the space originally assigned them in the felt factory and had been moved to the upper loft. Finally, what had been the stables on Dolge Avenue were turned into a shoe factory in 1891 (now factory #1). Dolge himself observed in a speech that year that "in reality, had we not had the shoe business we would have been really hard up for work." Concerning the lumber business he said, "One remarkable thing I have to report . . . that for the first time in twelve years our lumber pilers have learned to put up a straight pile of lumber and it is no longer offensive to the eye of a mechanic, or any one with notions of symmetry and straight lines to go through our lumber yards." Ever concerned with diversity, he reported, "Something has turned up this year which promises to keep the lumber department in good humor for some time to come—the piano-case making."[13]

A Herkimer County historian has described the lumber operations at Leipzig, where a German-trained forester named Julius Linz lived in a house built specially for him and was in charge of sawing operations: "A small army of men cut out the trees into four foot wood which was dried and sawn by teams in winter to feed the boilers of the Dolge Mills. . . . Houses were built and soon there was a thriving village 'way back in the solid forest. A gravity railroad, with flanged wheels, running on poles in place of iron rails, drew out from this region hundreds of thousands of logs. Millions of feet of lumber were stacked up to season and later to be drawn to the sounding board mill or to market by a long string of teams."[14]

The woods used to make the piano cases and moldings included such native ones as ash, oak, cherry, rock maple, and walnut, in addition to rosewood and mahogany, which had to be imported. Six big molding machines worked automatically; as many as four thousand knives were used in some of the patterns.

As a result of all this, there were other improvements. The roads were better. Representatives of Steinway, Aeolian, Gulbrandson, Kronig, and Bach who came to buy felt or sounding boards now found plenty of hotels to patronize. The streets around the factory were lighted at night. And before long, one more industry would arrive in Dolgeville.

Franz Joseph Brambach had opened his first piano factory at Bonn, Germany in 1823. In 1880 the company moved to New York. In 1890 it moved to Dolgeville. The first complete piano was produced there in 1892. From then on, the plan called for a total of three thousand a year.[15]

In 1891 the village was incorporated with Alfred Dolge its first president. The year 1892 saw the completion of a railroad line to Dolgeville—a tremendous development and an inducement to new industry.

In 1893, Dolge exhibited his piano felts and sounding boards at the World's Columbian Exhibition in Chicago as he had done in Vienna in 1873, at Philadelphia in 1876, and once again at the Paris Exposition of 1878. As in the past, his products received "the highest awards, six in number."[16] He could make felt, no doubt about that. He could also sell it, if not always at a profit.

The year 1893 saw other developments—some of them favorable, some not. A newly built woolen factory, with Dolge's brother Hugo in charge, burned down. On the other hand, an unusual new industry arrived that year—the making of an instrument known as the autoharp, which had originated with the C. F. Zimmerman Company of Philadelphia. Intrigued by its sweet, guitar-like tone, Alfred Dolge brought the factory to Dolgeville and put it in what had been the *Turnverein* clubhouse, with his son Rudolf in charge. Nationally advertised, and featured by Victor Herbert, it sold for $4 up to $150 at the Dolge Building on East 13th Street in New York.[17] Eventually almost every attic in Dolgeville contained an autoharp or two. Though it was popular in some places—especially the Southern Appalachians, where it became a folk instrument—it never swept the country. But it has never completely disappeared.

By now Dolge was making yearly trips abroad. During one of his visits to Germany he had spent some time with members of the Giese family, whose piano wire he had been importing. Made under a patented process that gave it added strength, the wire was especially well suited for the upright pianos that had now come into vogue. As a result of Dolge's interest, Rudolph Giese in his turn paid a visit to Dolgeville to consider opening a factory there. Deciding that the foundation work should be done in Germany and the finishing in the United States, Giese left his younger brothers Herman and Ernst in charge, and in 1893 the Giese Wire Company opened a factory in Dolgeville. The Little Falls *Journal and Courier* described the newcomers in 1895 as "two big stalwart men, typically German in build and complexion, and with that energy which has made so many natives of the Fatherland so successful in business in the United States."

Dolge's own venture in wire making was less happy. Dr. Carlton Spofford, a dentist by training, was put in charge and ten or fifteen men were employed. But there was a clash of temperaments, and after a disagreement over the teaching of German in public schools the project came to a disagreeable end.[18]

Relations with William Menge, an immigrant from Germany, were more satisfactory. Menge had arrived in the United States in 1882 after twenty-four days on an old wooden ship; he had paid thirty dollars' fare, food included. A skilled mechanic—he had begun his career as a blacksmith's apprentice, working twelve hours a day for board and lodging. He soon found work with the Singer Sewing Machine Company. He was living in Troy, where he had migrated with his family on the Hudson River Boat Line, when in 1894 he saw an advertisement for a machinist in Dolgeville and decided to try his luck in a community where German was spoken. English was still such a foreign language to him that once, when he was actually being congratulated for fine work, he thought he was being fired. As a maker of presses and hammers for Alfred Dolge, Menge in time was employing eight or nine men in his own machine shop.[19]

Newcomers from Germany continued to arrive in Dolgeville. More than once a lonesome German boy, wandering the streets of New York, would discover the office of Alfred Dolge and, recognizing the name for a German one, go in and apply for work. Such a boy was Paul Frederick Thomas. The youngest of seven children, he had been fourteen when his older brother wrote from New York urging his mother to send Paul over. Without waiting to write anything in reply, Paul left at once, traveling in steerage. He landed in Baltimore with a friend, Ernest, who went with him to New York to look for the older brother. The landlady who came to the door spoke German, and she gave Paul the heartbreaking news that his brother had gone to Wisconsin. Though Ernest by then had a ticket that would take him upstate, he offered to stay with Paul. But Paul persuaded his friend that he could manage, pointing out that he had money in his pocket (it amounted to seventy-five cents) whereas Ernest had only his ticket. A kindly butcher gave him a job and a home for nine years; then, having made up his mind that he would not be a butcher for the rest of his life, Paul Thomas read a sign advertising for help in the window of Alfred Dolge (which sounded German to him) and proceeded upstate to Dolgeville. He became a stitcher, and in his spare time he became expert at fencing. Small and dark, he was so agile with sabre and foils that his German friends, with typical humor, nicknamed him the "Cockroach." When a slipper box factory was added to the Dolge enterprises, Paul Thomas was put in charge.[20]

Another young German, Paul Franz, had been preceded to Dolgeville by his father, a skilled harnessmaker who had heard of the Dolge industries in Germany and had gone there to make way for the rest of his family. He became a shoemaker there. Paul arrived in New York in 1885, on the day of General Grant's funeral—an occasion he mistook for some kind of holiday. He traveled upstate with mixed feelings. Having read the *Leatherstocking Tales* of James Fenimore Cooper in Germany, he half expected to find an Indian behind every tree. What he found instead was a small apartment in a row of attached houses that Dolge had built for his employees. The place was crowded, and Paul soon went to live with the Timmerman family on a farm that was part of the old Palatine settlement near Snell's Bush, south of Dolgeville. The Timmermans were good to him, and helped him with his English. People who knew him then described him as tall, slender, and merry.[21] He became a designer in the slipper factory ("Hi-Lo" and "Comfy" slippers were his specialty) and eventually its superintendent.

In August 1895, Alfred Dolge spoke at the 125th anniversary of the Palatine Church in the town of Palatine. His theme was the men who had transplanted their skills and their culture to the region that was now his home. "Finally," he said, "the great exodus of 1848–50 brought to our shores the very best elements the Fatherland had produced in a century. These men, farmers, mechanics, professionals, artists, and scholars had profited from Germany's greatest period of intellectual activity. They had been reared under the influence of the great poets, Goethe, Schiller, Heine, and the philosophers Kant, Hegel, Fichte, Schopenhauer; the composers, Mozart, Weber, Haydn, Beethoven; and those great educators Pestalozzi and Frederick Froebel."

Whether he knew it or not, he could have been describing himself. He was also describing the men he had recruited for an enterprise that was in many ways unique.

In the crashing clarity of the autumn colors, the blue of the softer seasons and the sharp cold of the frozen northern winter the Dutchmen would move in their great coats and their fur caps, building a life.

CHAPTER 3

REFORMER AND INNOVATOR

On his yearly trips to Europe, Alfred Dolge continued to take note of the low wages there.[1] In 1888, a man working twelve hours a day might earn thirty and a half cents, and a woman as little as twenty cents. His continued reading of works on economics, in both English and German, gave him further incentive to find a solution to the problem of labor in his own factories. The efforts of Fourier in France, of the Rochdale Society in England, and the Brook Farm and the Oneida Community in America aroused his imagination, and his sympathies were engaged by the conditions he found at Brockett's Bridge.[2] Soon after the arrival of 1,700 Germans in the village, an epidemic of typhoid fever broke out as a result of the proximity of wells and outhouses. The immigrants were crowded into boarding houses where they slept on the floor, several families to a building. The houses were inadequately heated by stoves and lighted with kerosene. As late as 1882, a fire that was probably caused by an overturned lantern had destroyed a large part of Main Street before a pumper could arrive from Little Falls.

Children went to work at the age of twelve or fourteen both in the factories and on the farms, and their earnings went to feed the rest of their families. Mothers often worked in the factories or sewed shoes at home. The diet was furnished largely by the surrounding countryside. It was monotonous in winter and varied only with the season; there might be venison, trout, maple syrup, greens, garden produce, berries and nuts, as well as pork or beef. Clothes were rough and homemade. Schooling stopped at the sixth grade. Once a family's savings ran out, there was nothing to fall back on in the event of misfortune except charity.

All this was typical of a small industrial town and not very different from immigrant life in a city tenement. In Dolgeville there came to be a difference which gradually transformed the village into a uniquely pleasant and lively place.

This was at a time when the Carnegies, the Rockefellers, the Vanderbilts, and the Fisks were building industrial empires. What Dolge built grew out of his determination that children should no longer scavenge coal, or old men wind up in paupers' graves. It was his belief that a workman should be able to retire at the age of sixty on a pension paid for by his employer as a part of the cost of production. The security of such a plan, he wrote, "would allow the laborer to live better and [be] more healthy, keep his wife home and his children in school. He could live up to his income and spend more thus developing a higher manhood and superior citizenship."[3] Dolge saw employees eventually becoming partners in a business, so that the capitalist would no longer be enriched at the expense of his laborers. Even though he believed in hard work as a way out of poverty, it was never his belief that the poor remained poor because of laziness. What he aimed for was in effect a leveling of the economy to benefit everyone rather than solely the man at the top.

No later than 1876, as soon as the felt-making factory was well established, Alfred Dolge set up a pension plan that was to remain almost unchanged as long as the business was his. The benefits ranged from 50 percent of wages for disability after ten years of service, up to 100 percent after twenty-five years. In the event of accident or sickness related to employment, 50 percent of wages were to be paid during the period of disability even without the completion of ten years as an employee.

Dolge added a life insurance plan for his employees, a second part of his threefold plan. Those with five years' service were guaranteed $1,000 worth of insurance; those with ten years got another thousand. There was, in addition, a Mutual Aid Society into which members earning $6 a week paid 50¢ a month, and those earning less than $6 paid 25¢ a month. In the event of sickness, benefits amounting to $5 a week for those in the first category, and $2.50 a week for those in the second, were to be paid. Those who retired because of chronic ailments or age would draw $1 a week in addition to their pensions, and $50 would be paid in death benefits. Finally, in 1890, a program of Earning-Sharing, the third part of Dolge's plan under which an employee received a percentage of earnings to be calculated according to the value of his contribution in brains or labor, was introduced. It called for an intricate system of bookkeeping, since the bonus amounts were credited to the employee and reinvested, and a loss was charged against him. The total thus earned was not turned over to the employee until the time of retirement. This proved to be one of his less successful experiments.[4]

The growing demand by the Knights of Labor and other groups for an eight-hour working day did not go unnoticed in Dolgeville. In 1886, when a series of strikes and the Haymarket Square riot in Chicago focused attention on the issue, Dolge's employees did not themselves go on strike but they did ask for a meeting to discuss it. As a result, the working day in his factories was cut from ten to nine hours. To explain why he could not reduce it to eight Dolge said "I would at once be compelled to cease manufacturing, as my customers would not pay me this immense difference, because the European felt can already be sold for less in our market than our cost of manufacturing."[5]

An opponent of free trade from the start, Dolge never ceased to point out the connection between the low price of imports and the starvation wages paid to the workers who produced them. Whereas an American mechanic earned $4 a day, for example, his European counterpart received only the equivalent of $1. Dolge also told of a meeting in Germany at which a reformer named Schultze Delitzsch, after demonstrating that a pound of buckwheat contained more nourishment than a pound of butter, declared that since buckwheat cost only 8¢ a pound, as compared to the 25¢ that butter cost, a working man could save a great deal of money simply by giving up butter and living entirely on buckwheat. When Delitzsch had finished his speech, a laboring man came to the platform. "Mr. Schultze Delitzsch is certainly correct," he began, "in saying that butter is dearer than buckwheat and that he would save money if he stopped eating it, but how far this theory is true and correct as to the ultimate effect I can prove to you if you will come with me to the manufacturing districts of Silesia. The workingmen there do not eat butter nor even buckwheat; they live on potatoes all the year round and hardly know meat by sight, and my friends, these frugal, saving work people can manage to lay up so much money that they and their children can afford to go barefooted all the year around." To this, Dolge added his own observation, that "the more frugally they lived, the more their wages were cut down. I think," he went on "this is quite apropo to the teachings of the Free Trader, who promises such a brilliant future for the workingman if he can buy everything so cheaply, but the Free Trader forgets that under free trade, wages will be so reduced that the workingman will hardly be able to buy food for his family."[6]

Dolge had no more patience with opponents of labor saving machinery. He added new machines to his own factories as fast as he could. To a man he met who argued that one machine could put twenty-nine men out of work, he gave this vehement reply: "You know, and every thinking man knows, that every labor saving machine invented is a boon for the laboring people of the world, because nature has not given us our brains that they should be idle and that we should trudge along in hard, muscle-consuming labor. We were not given brains to work like the horse or ox in a treadmill, day after day, without knowing why and what we produce, but nature has given us our brains for the purpose that we should use the same to ascertain how to curtail the work, the labor of our hands, and the more brains that are put into performance of our duties the less hours it will take us."[7]

Dolge also continually linked labor with education, arguing for reforms that would guarantee the education of employees. If this were done, he said, "We should have a class of workingmen, intelligent and industrious, who would, because of their intelligence, produce in eight hours as much as we can produce in ten; men who would know how to save and take care of their earnings over and above what they need for food and clothing."[8]

Besides concerning himself with economics, Alfred Dolge was soon finding ways to offset the immigrant's natural loneliness and to lighten the hard life of readjustment with social events and physical exercise. Physical fitness was part of his vision of a model community. By 1885 a gymnasium and clubhouse had come into existence to accommodate the newly organized *Turnverein*, a club that combined gymnastic exercise with social gatherings reminiscent of the youth club Dolge had founded in Leipzig so many years before. That year, at the first picnic of the new organization, he issued this invitation to fitness: "Come to the Club House half an hour after your supper, young men, and jump over the bars and lines, or swing on the rings, and I guarangee you that you will sleep the sleep of the innocent and that no exciting dreams or nightmares will deprive you of your needed rest. But you must go at it in dead earnest and stick to it, not for one week, or one month, or one year only, for ten years or more, as long as you are limber enough to keep it up. You must not consider it your only aim to jump with wonted éclat and elegance over the horizontal bar, and then be satisfied if you can show off well at a public exhibition."

Dolge believed that in a town so isolated, with its long winters, people should be encouraged to relax and enjoy themselves. "Drink some lager beer," he said, "and have sociable songs with fresh vigor, and we go to work again next morning, joyfully and gladly."[9] Concerning music he observed, "Wherever you hear music you find culture, taste, the nobler instincts of mankind more or less developed."[10] To bring music to Dolgeville, he organized a festival known as the *Maennerchor*, which drew singers from Albany, Rochester and Syracuse. In announcing one festival, with 500 expected to come, a notice in the *Dolgeville Herald* urged the townspeople to open their homes to the visitors, some of whom were "older, staid, and married people accustomed to regularity, past the time when a rollicking night is enjoyed."[11]

The *Dolgeville Herald* had begun publication in July 1888, another of Alfred Dolge's projects, and a typically ambitious one. It had twenty employees, and he had persuaded Van Cullen Jones, an experienced newspaperman who had been with Robert Lewis Stevenson in Samoa, to come up from New York to serve as its editor. The paper became a vehicle not only for advertisements but also for reaching a public beyond Dolgeville itself with Dolge's ideas on profit sharing and pensions, as well as cultural reform and the question of free trade versus the protective tariff.

His theories were drawing attention both at home and abroad.[12] In 1889, according to his own account, the government of France requested a detailed account of his pension plan. So did the German government; eventually a plan much like it was adopted there. In the United States, ironically, progress was to be much slower. By 1930, in fact, no more than 100,000 of the millions of American workingmen had any protection against unemployment.[13]

He went on puzzling over the workings of the economy. As agriculture gave way to industry, he saw that the ideas of the old authorities, Adam Smith, David Ricardo, John Stuart Mill, no longer applied. The old formula that "profits rise as wages fall, and fall as wages rise," he discarded as inhuman. On the other hand, the doctrine of Marx that labor was entitled to all the profit, was equally repugnant to him.[14] His feelings on this subject came out in a statement he made to his employees: "I wish you all understand that neither with the starting fund of the aid society, nor with the pension fund, nor this life insurance plan, I mean to offer you a gift or a present. I consider you are entitled to it as a part of your earnings, as your share of the profits which the business yields and which I only invest for you. If I make presents for you they come in the shape of this clubhouse, or in the shape of more volumes to your library, which I hope you will accept and make good use of."[15]

A strong supporter of the Republican party, Dolge became interested in marshalling the German vote. During the campaign of 1892, he organized a large rally of German-American Republicans, their first gathering of any size in seventeen years, at Cooper Union in New York City. He never ran for office, but contented himself with promoting his beliefs in this way and through the press.[16]

The *Turnfest* had become an annual celebration, and the highest prize, "a wreath made of plain maple leaves by fair hands," was a coveted one.[17] Dolgeville residents had become skilled on the horizontal bar, in club swinging by both women and men, and in fencing with broadsword and foils. There were literary contests as well. The most elaborate of these festivals, in July 1894, brought a crowd of 10,000. Five hundred *Turners* from New York were quartered in the Brambach piano factory. There was an orchestra, along with three bands: the Little Falls Military Band, the Dolgeville Brass and Reed band, and the Dolgeville Drum and Fife corps. Arches reading *Gut Heil* ("Good Health") and *Wilkommen* went up at the entrances to the town and buildings were trimmed in red, white, and blue. Nine trains a day arrived from Little Falls, and the festival went on from Wednesday until Saturday, with a ball every evening. Five hundred marchers paraded through the streets, including some ladies in divided skirts (the only mention of Bloomer Girls ever found in Dolgeville). A rocket and an elephant balloon were sent up.[18] A few minor casualties were reported. Two elderly men were riding the merry-go-round at High Falls Park when the cutter in which they were seated came loose, and they barely escaped being thrown to the ground (it was said that the hair of both men turned white as a result). Only three horses of spectators bolted, luckily without loss of life or limb.

Commemorative steins, issued for the occasion adorned every stump and platform in the grove where the kaleidoscope of merrymaking took place.[19] A beautiful wooded natural amphitheater, where the High Falls spilled down a glacier-carved ravine, contained little summerhouses built by the Germans, connected by paths that made walking easier. For the occasion the buildings were aflutter with flags and bunting. Tables spread with white cloths had been set with a variety of rich foods and steins of dark beer. Swings dipped and lifted, the merry-go-round wheezed away, the bands piped, and throngs of women in long sweeping skirst and men in sailor straws intermingled with at least a thousand excited children moved about the grounds.

Rosa Freygang years later recalled the occasion. Her dark hair drawn neatly up into a crown, her long black dress covered by a spotless white apron, she had been up since dawn, preparing food for the Turners. She remembered that they had requested sauerbraten and potato dumplings for their heavy meal (a three-day job when done correctly). "I told them, no," she said firmly, the appealing little click still in her accent. "Und the potato dumplings—vell you take these little knitted bags I brought from Germany, und you put it at once into the bags und run water fresh and cold through them to whiten it, und you squeeze them, und *squeeze* them until they are dry, und you mix in cold mashed potatoes und seasonings und little fried bits of bread und shape them und then you dust them, und put them quick like in bubbling fresh water, but it must not boil, but only be between a simmer und a boil on the back of the stove, vell, I couldn't give it to them!"

All day, nevertheless, Rosa helped at the open fires, serving the men wursts and salads and hot slaws, along with coffee and beer. At the end of the day, Alfred Dolge himself called her to the stage. She went up blushing and twisting her apron, to be awarded a diploma for her work in preparing the dinners. It was not a great pleasure to her, she recalled. She was too tired.[20]

Things were not uniformly cheerful in Dolgeville that year. It was in 1894 that for the first time in twenty-five years, the factories in Dolgeville stopped running. Dolge had been obliged to close them down for lack of orders, due largely, he believed, to uncertainty over the tariff.[21]

Nevertheless, social life went on as as before. A skating club was organized, with Dolge as its honorary president. There was a membership fee of two dollars; a lighted house and heated benches were provided. A roller skating rink had been laid out in the Turnhall, on Elm Street. To replace the Turnhall there was a new and more elaborate social club, complete with a library and reading rooms in addition to space for bowling and billiards, the gynmasium, and an auditorium with the finest stage in the Mohawk Valley.[22] Many of the Germans were naturally athletic, and Dolge encouraged them to excel. Paul Thomas, years afterward, recalled the agility he had developed on the horizontal bars. Walter Menge thought nothing at the time of cycling to Schenectady and back, a journey of fifty miles each way, and he skated until he was in his eighties. In the Turnhall, the Germans danced the waltz and the schottische with great whirls and turns. Banquets, balls, and concerts were popular.[23] Guests wearing evening dress arrived in horse-drawn carriages. Watching the departures after one particularly sumptuous occasion, as was reported in the November 21, 1895 *Herald*, Dolge said with a flourish of his ever present cigar, "In twenty years from a wilderness hamlet, by factories and education to this!"

The occasion was a concert by Gilmore's Band, led by Victor Herbert, the sort of concert that was seldom performed except in cities with a population of at least 15,000. There had been a somewhat embarrassing hitch, it is true, a power failure that occurred just as the final round of applause began, plunging musicians and an audience of a thousand into darkness. Luckily, the power came on again in time for the reception Alfred Dolge had prepared at the splendid new house into which he had moved his family only a few months before.

The town was not, of course, the model community that Dolge continued to envision. The hours were still long. Many still began work at the age of fourteen. Even the younger children had work to do. They carried home-sewn shoes to the factory, helped with chores, or picked up coal from the tracks. Strictly disciplined, they were admonished to be seen and not heard—particularly at mealtimes, when they were to speak only when addressed by an elder. The women were expected to stay at home, but if the family needed money there was work for them in the factories. Often the men of the household ate first, the wives and children afterward. More than one boy ran away rather than turn over his entire weekly pay to the family. Nevertheless, there was much close family feeling, and the men were devoted husbands and fathers. For the children, there were games such as Fox and Geese on a Board and Skittles.[24] For the women, there were kaffee klatches where they lingered over fancy work and gossip until, regretfully, they had to leave and "make" dinner at home.

The Yankees of the town were astonished by some German practices they considered outlandish. A German mother got a talking-to from a neighbor for giving beer to her children. "Well you give pie to yours," was the reply.[25]

Though Alfred Dolge wrote hopefully of mingling all nationalities at the Turnhall, the gatherings there remained typically German. But he did not give up promoting either gymnastics or music, despite some raised eyebrows in a village that had previously known, by way of entertainment, mainly hop pickings, square dances, and roof-raising bees. In his own words, "I invited my New York friends, among the leading musicians, to spend part of their summer vacation at Dolgeville and arrange with their assistance concerts, which in the beginning were free. Soon thereafter the first piano made its appearance in the home of a workman, which was followed by many more later on. A desire for higher culture awakened to such an extent that I could risk the engagement of prominent musical organizations such as Victor Herbert's band, the New York Philharmonic Club and others to give concerts in Dolgeville, which was rather remarkable for a village up in the mountains with about 3,000 inhabitants."[26]

Indeed, all this was quite new to upstate New York. The bilingual village with its concerts and parties, the taste for luxury that was being cultivated, did not escape the notice of observers in neighboring places, who came, saw, and went home to ponder what was happening. Money was being made in Dolgeville—quite possibly by some who did not understand the ramifications of finance in their adopted country.

Alfred Dolge. Carte de visite, circa 1868. (Photograph by Naegeli, New York City.)

Anna Dolge. Carte de visite, circa 1868. (Photograph by August Brasch, Leipzig.)

Stereoscopic view of the Dolge residence on Dolge Avenue in 1882 (before the addition of the 1886 mansard).

Alfred Dolge factory, 1888. (Photograph by Ernst Knabe, Jr.)

Alfred and Anna Dolge circa 1886. (Photographs by Naegeli, New York City.)

The Dolge residence decorated for the twenty-first Turnfest, August 18, 1888 (photograph by Ernst Knabe, Jr.).

Wedding train and guests of Rudolf Dolge and his bride, Anita Heller-Schneller, March 16, 1893. Rudolf, in the foreground, wears a bowler.

The Alfred Dolge Hose Co., No. 1. From the souvenir program of the November 1897 Dolgeville Fair and Bazaar.

"Two Republicans. An Object Lesson For Our Manufacturers." Cartoon

from *Truth*, August 6, 1892.

Alfred Dolge's Christmas card from Covina, California, 1908.

Alfred and Anna Dolge with friends in the Harz Mountains, 1921.

CHAPTER 4
GEMÜTLICHKEIT

Alfred Dolge had brought his family from New York to Brockett's Bridge. His firstborn, Rudolf, born in 1869, was followed by William, 1876, Henry in in 1883, Ernst in 1884, and Fritz in 1885. Their first home in the village was a solid Victorian house on Main Street, across from the felt factory. Encircled by a porch, it had added a mansard roof by 1886. Later there was a fountain in its small front yard.

It was not long before other members of the clan were added to the growing population. Christian August Dolge, by now a gray-bearded *Grossvater*, arrived from Germany in 1880, was tendered a great reception, and took up residence in a farmhouse on Dolge Avenue, overlooking the river. Of his six children, three others settled in Dolgeville: his sons Henry and Hugo, who became Alfred's associates in the business, and his daughter Anna and her husband, Gustav Guenther, who lived with him. The others were Bruno in New York and Selma (Mrs. Fred Engelhart) in St. Johnsville. The farmhouse became a gathering place for the entire family. Here on a summer afternoon you might find Alfred, Henry, Hugo and their wives and children sitting about a picnic table spread with a linen cloth under the blue sky. With pipes and steins of beer and good talk, the brothers passed many pleasant hours, often in the company of a group of friends who called themselves the German Club.

The farmhouse was a little outside the village, and *Grossvater* found space there for a menagerie of pets—prairie dogs, coyotes, raccoons (known to the Germans as "washbears," and a favorite with visitors for their endearing traits), owls, and even an eagle. Their cages lined the road below the farm, and nearby was a five-acre fenced area where deer, wild geese, peacocks, and guinea fowl were kept. Lumberjacks often brought the young of wild creatures to old Mr. Dolge, and he and his daughter Anna bottle fed many of them. Among them were two bears, known as Schnippsal and Schnappsal, who followed their foster parents about the farm and even into the village, where they so frightened the horses that a den was constructed to keep them from wandering. It contained a shelter and was surrounded by a blue stone wall, fifteen feet high and eighteen inches thick, surmounted by steel spikes eight inches apart. On a tree stump in the midst of the den, the bears' antics could be observed and rewarded with sugar.

Grossvater Dolge took a great interest in an island in East Canada Creek where there was a stand of first-growth pines. A wooden bridge was built to connect it with Dolge Avenue, and it came to be known as *Bratwurst Insel* or "Sausage Island." Here, in addition to the wiener roasts that gave the island its name, there were dances, plays and music festivals or *Gesangfests*. An open-air dance floor was lighted by oil lanterns. The dancing was usually accompanied by a hand organ or an accordion, but sometimes there was an orchestra.[1] Emogene Bliss recalled the scene years later: "My, how those Germans used to dance stout [hard]!"[2] But tastes are fickle. By 1885 the wiener roasting grills, the bridge and dance floor had been abandoned, alas, and the pine trees cut down.

Much as Christian Dolge regretted the passing of the island, he was never at a loss for new projects. One day he suggested to Alfred that the scrub-covered hill behind the farmhouse might be planted to trees. Alfred was pleased with the idea—besides adding an improvement, it would give work to men who had been laid off because business was slack. The place became known as Summer House Hill, and in time an open-air pavilion was built there. Paths and picnic spots were laid out among the rows of oak, maple, birch, and pine, and space was cleared around the natural springs. In winter there was a lighted toboggan slide. And at the foot of the hill, three ponds were stocked with carp and bullheads—another of the old man's projects.

Herbert Guenther has described the seining of the ponds, which became an annual occasion: "Once every year, generally late fall, the water was partly drained, and the ponds seined. The largest fish, some five to eight pounds, were removed and placed in fish boxes located in the East Canada Creek above the factory dam for winter consumption. The small fry were returned to the ponds.

Seining the ponds was a real occasion for many of *Grossvater*'s friends and other visitors. The project required fifteen or twenty men to handle the large nets which spanned from shore to shore. A group of men were required on each shore and three men in a boat took care of the leaded underline in the pond. At that time of the year it was always cold (carp were considered fit to eat only when the water was near freezing) so a roaring shore fire was built, the material for which had been gathered for weeks.

Stacks of various kinds of sandwiches, hot dogs, and rolls, and a hot drink called *warme beer*, made of beer, milk, eggs, lemon peel, and spices, was plentiful. This drink sounds awful but when made and served piping hot is a splendid warmer on a cold day. No money was ever paid for helping at this fish festival, in fact it was considered an honor to be invited to participate, but everyone that helped went home with a good mess of fish. In the winter the pond was kept clear of snow for skating."[3]

Henry Dolge, who had been in the real estate business in New York, took charge of the Dolge lumber mills in 1882. Around 1885 he began developing High Falls Park, the scene of many *Turnfests.* He had his own trout ponds there, and was responsible for the covered dancing pavilion, the bandstand, ball diamond, swings, and picnic tables, and the "Lovers' Walk" to the canyon of the High Falls in East Canada Creek. The four trains a day that ran from Little Falls to Dolgeville often held fifty or more visitors when there was a special occasion; horse buses holding fifteen or twenty people would be there to meet the train and transport them to the park. The last two visitors to climb aboard would have the task of holding the door closed.[4] On the Fourth of July 1890, according to one report, there was lager beer in abundance; one could, "if diligent enough, contrive to locate a glass of water."[5]

Alfred Dolge's own household had continued to grow. Fritz, the youngest of his five sons, had been born and by then Alfred had begun to envision the new house for his family that would go up near the site of the farmhouse. Christian Dolge and the Guenther family moved into the house on Main Street and work began on what was to be a beautiful home of Queen Anne architecture. Spires, dormers, and mansard roofs were already to be seen rising above the modest storefronts and farmhouses of the original village, as mansions belonging to the Gieses, the Horns, the Armstrongs, the Amanns, the Breckwoldts, and still others were built. Never had wood been used more lavishly; lofty ceilings, large rooms, open arches, and pier glass mirrors confirmed that money was indeed being made at Dolgeville.

On July 25, 1895, the *Dolgeville Herald* reported that "A. Dolge" had "moved into his new residence on Dolge Avenue." For his Anna he had built the kingliest house in the village; it was almost a *Schloss.* Two years in the building, it had employed German cabinet-makers, Swiss woodcarvers, and Italian plasterers, and among its features were $10,000 worth of paneling and brass doorknobs worth $1,800.[6] There were forty rooms, plus stables and greenhouses. The bathrooms were decorated with pansies—Anna Dolge's favorite flower. Behind the house were a terrace and rock gardens—the rock specially imported from Italy. Freda Cunningham, who had been a maid in the Dolges' old house, remembered that Anna was an avid gardener, who cared for the plants in the conservatory herself, spraying the leaves and washing the jars in the kitchen. As Freda described the house, "In one room a New York artist had painted the wall, and there were beautiful paintings in the house. Blue willow ware dishes were used, and the music room had a cabinet of beautiful dishes. There was a state dining room, a tower with a billiard room, and sleeping rooms."

Freda had gone to work for the Dolges when she was sixteen and earned eight dollars a month. "I was on my knees most of the time. I'd never been on my knees so much in my life," Freda said. Nevertheless, she was devoted to Anna Dolge. "She was a very, very nice lady, very bright, friendly, tall, not too stout, and carried herself nicely. She was dark, dark."[7]

Another maid was Sophie Goebel, who answered the "Help Wanted" sign in the New York window. As a young girl she had come from the province of Hesse, with her three sisters and two brothers. She was in her twenties when she came to Dolgeville—a bright, capable girl, good at needlework and knitting and intricate cut work, who could be trusted to care for small children. When Hugo Dolge was left a widower with two small children, Anna suggested she join that household, beginning what was to be a lifetime career as a children's nurse.[8]

Other servants in the household, Freda Cunningham recalled, were a housekeeper who had been with the family for many years, a cook, a dining room girl and a kitchen helper. "I didn't see Alfred Dolge enough to know him during the two years I was there," Freda said. "He had a New York office, and the coachman met him at the train with a sleigh in winter."[9]

It was Anna who ran the household. She had a budget of $6,000 a year and entertained constantly as businessmen and their wives, with other guests from New York, continued to arrive. Occasionally she would travel abroad with her husband. She spoke of him as "all that a man should be." He believed in strict discipline, and brought up his sons to be gentlemen. In the big new house, the lively boys slept on the top floor, on old beds; there were rag rugs on the floor. Several of the maids testified that they loved to tease.

At parties in the new house, invited guests were expected to exchange their shoes for felt slippers when dancing to keep the parquet floors in perfect condition Dr. Wendell Bowman later related.

By the time the new house was ready, Rudolf was twenty-six and already a married man. Henry was said to be interested only in sports. William was just back from a tour of the South on his bicycle, and Ernst, a student in a military school at Cornwall-on-Hudson, worked in the machine shop during his vacation.[10] While Rudolf was expected to be taking an interest in the business, Fritz was too young to direct. Rudolf's frail health at this time was a matter of concern to Alfred Dolge. It had necessitated a walking tour of the South and two years in Europe. When one boy lost an eye, Alfred suffered terribly for him. Otherwise he appeared composed; whatever worries the business gave him, he kept to himself. Neither his weekly trips to New York nor his yearly trips to Europe could interfere with his voluminous reading or writing or with his continual involvement in community affairs.

December 22, 1893 was Alfred and Anna's twenty-fifth wedding anniversary, and it was celebrated with family and friends. There was now an Alfred, Jr., Rudolf's son, born in 1893 and the object of some humor when they said the name of such a little boy seriously interfered with the trademark. In typed manuscripts of the speeches delivered at the party, Alfred's is memorable because it reveals his relationship with his wife, which was mutually supportive according to other guests.

Speaking of Anna he said, "It was those black eyes that spurred me on and six months after that ball (where they met) I made up my mind to go to America. (They had made no pledges but carried on a lively correspondence.) In two years I returned to Germany for four months. At that time it was again understood without saying anything that we should go through life together. The only keepsake I had was a picture of the jet black eyes presented by the owner."

He had returned to America and went on, "When she arrived, she was perfectly composed. She went to the plain boarding house where my brother was living. She wore a dark dusty dress of the crossing. The landlady gave her a bonnet, white, but three sizes too large, meaning well!"

They gave $2 to the minister and a few hours later they took a boat for New Haven where they lived six months. Alfred earned good wages here but when they returned to New York, Anna did all the work for eight boarders for two years going beyond her strength, but always cheerful for she was earning house rent and expenses. "A year later she had to go to Germany to recover her health which she had lost through overwork. She stayed there for a number of years and when she came back she was a mature woman. . . . Our five boys' . . . physical and moral condition they owe entirely to their mother. . . . Drink with me to the praise of the woman whose life is love, and whose love is life."

Once he and his household were settled in the new mansion, the old house on Main Street became a hotel, the Guenther House, with Alfred's sister Anna and her husband in charge. It was the scene of many parties. Fine food was in abundance. Anniversaries were marked by lavish gifts, such as a "bride's wreath and groom's bouquet in solid silver from 'A.D.' cake and coffee service from Mrs. A. Dolge." Often the effervescent Grosspapa Dolge would give a speech. Among the early guests at the Guenther House whose names are on record were Hugo Dolge, Herman Giese, E. R. Wanckel, and Sergei Rasterajef of St. Petersburg. Others came from Dresden and Berlin, and from as far away as Australia. Members of Gilmore's Band and the Fallis Orchestra of Little Falls, who played for the Turners' masked ball, inscribed their names in the Guenther House register. So did some pranksters—Gib Lets from the Stock Yard and Hans Stick-in-the-Mud from New Jersey on the Rhine—who checked in at 4:30 a.m. after what must have been a jolly evening.[12]

For all the luxury and entertainment Alfred Dolge had brought to Dolgeville, his boys were brought up to revel in the out of doors, at no more than one remove from genuine hardship. Ernst recalled returning from military school on a winter night when the temperature dropped to thirty or more degrees below zero, and being met by two servants in an open sleigh drawn by "Old Bob." If his father, who had so often walked the eight miles from Little Falls to Dolgeville when the snowbanks towered above his head, could stand the cold, then so could he.[13]

Some of the Teutonic religion, with its forest altars, perhaps lingered in these German's love of the wilderness. They hunted there, and their wives made sauerbraten of the venison, or roasted the bear meat. Alfred Dolge knew the region well from his travels through the Adirondacks in search of timber. One day in June, 1892, he was relaxing at John Breckwoldt's camp, which stood on a point between the East and West Canada Lakes, an ideal spot for catching both sunrise and sunset as they were reflected in the glimmering waters. With Dolge and Breckwoldt were Lou Snell and another whose name has been forgotten. They had been playing cards on the porch. At the end of a hand, Alfred Dolge got up to stretch and light a cigar. He looked out over the expanse, one of the most stunning in the Adirondacks. "Boys," he said quietly, "I've just bought the Canada Lakes."[14]

The investment was not altogether a surprise. His companions knew that many able businessmen had been acquiring land in the region, building mills, tanneries, and hotels, and that some were ready to sell. On that day, June 17, 1892, Alfred Dolge had contracted to buy from former Governor Claffin of Massachusetts and two others a total of 4,600 acres of land and water.[15] By 1896, his holdings around the five lakes had been increased to over 40,000 acres.[16]

Alfred Dolge's interest in the Adirondack forests was partly commercial, but it was something more than that. "Even before I became interested in the lumber business," he wrote, "the wholesale destruction of the forests by the lumbermen and tanners caused me great regret. This indiscriminate and wanton cutting of tiber is no more nor less than a public calamity."[17]

As long ago as 1883, Dolge's views had been sought by the Superintendent of the Adirondack Survey, Verplanck Colvin. Dolge replied that he did not favor state ownership of the forests, but rather a planned harvest from privately owned lands, similar to that in Germany but not quite so completely controlled. On advice of a trained *Oberforester*, a graduate of the German Tharandt Forest Academy, whom he hired to study the climate and soil as well as the timber itself, Dolge cut only mature trees, and directed that the discarded top branches were to be burned during the winter so as to avoid danger of forest fires. Dolge advocated "preservation of the forests of the Adirondack region as a source of water supply from the Hudson and other streams of the eastern and northern sections of this state." And he urged that trees along streams be left standing, as a further safeguard against erosion. He was maddened by the timber thieves who plagued the region—cutting fiddle butts from the best part of the trees, "leaving the balance, after cutting, to dry up and rot in the woods, thus furnishing fuel for the devouring element."[18] Some of the fiddle butts were taken from virgin stands; some were stolen from Dolge's own land, and were then sold to his own factories. He was thus all the more concerned about finding some way for the state to enforce the laws against stealing timber.

In 1884 Dolge was urging the construction of more railroads to give better access to the lumber. Two years before, in 1882, he had subscribed $10,000 toward the project of building a railroad from Little Falls to Dolgeville. In 1892, after several false starts, it finally went into operation. His determination to see it through had left him heavily in debt. But Dolge's enthusiasm for new projects was not deterred easily or for long.

In 1897 he built a new dam at Stewart's Landing, on the Canada Lakes, to form a reservoir so that power could be produced the year round—enough to light a city of 30,000. To celebrate the later opening of the Dolgeville power station, there was a banquet in 1898 in the state dining room of the Dolges' mansion, with Lieutenant Governor Aldrich as one of the guests.

Dolge had still other plans for the Canada Lakes, including a real estate development. In 1897 a prospectus for the Auskerada Park Club was sent to a list of possible investors. In glowing terms it described the five lakes, the fish and game, and the healthful aspects of the place. The club was to be limited to five hundred shares; each purchaser of a share would be required to buy one lake-front lot. "The purpose of the organizers" was "to accept as members none but a class of gentlemen whose reputations are beyond question; business and professional men of influence and standing." Income was to come from the timber on the 4,600 acres on which the option was held. The lakes were very easy to approach from the Little Falls and Dolgeville Railroad: following a ten mile drive to the inlet, a steamer would carry the passenger to the Auskerada Hotel or the Kanaughta House at the extreme eastern end. Mr. George Seidel, a graduate of the best European school of forestry, was to be chief forester. The corresponding secretary of the enterprise was named as William R. Blood, at 28 East 23rd Street in New York City.

"Not the least beautiful feature of these lakes," the brochure concluded, "are the shores that surround them, sloping gently upwards from the waters' edge, covered with acres of pinxters. These bushes are covered with a profusion of blooms, varying in color from the most delicate shade of pink to the deepest carmine. Against the background of green and brown the effect is marvelously pretty."[19]

Perhaps it was while the pinxters were in bloom that Alfred Dolge first conceived the project. Or was it the white nosegays of the witch hopple that inspired him? "When the witch hopple blossoms, spring has come," they say in the Adirondacks.[20] Dolge never built a cottage there, but he often brought summer visitors from New York and Dolgeville to Stewart's Landing along a corduroy road which had been used in colonial times. From there, before a launch or steamer was in operation, they would row the three miles to Canada Lake, pulling at their oars while herons with their long prehistoric profiles flew overhead and the queer laughing shriek of the loon followed them.

The names of Dolge and his guests are inscribed in the old cottage ledgers. Fall was a favorite season. The paisley colors spread over the mountains and in the mornings white frost lay on the leaf cups where they had been plucked from the trees as though by a giant hand. The flaunting red of the sumach, the royal purple of the late asters and the staunch brown of the oaks endeared the country to them. Some of Dolge's last really happy hours were spent under the spell of the witchery of the old, great mountains.

"They'd put up a platform and have their beer and dance anyplace," one little old lady said of the transplanted Germans.[21] There is a story of how, after a hotel was finally established at Canada Lake a German band rowed up from Stewart's Landing, instruments shining and uniforms a-twinkle and consumed quantities of beer and schnapps. On the way home, towed by the steamer in a string of rowboats they were so splashed that they had to bail out the boats with their instruments to stay afloat.[22]

By the time that hotel was built, Alfred Dolge was no longer on the scene at Dolgeville. He was in debt, and his affairs had grown increasingly tangled. But he was sanguine by temperament, and whatever worries he had he kept to himself. The Germans had a saying, "He wears an oak leaf on his shoulder"[23]—their way of describing a man of spirit and fortitude. Dolge wore the oak leaf.

Before the Germans came to Brockett's Bridge, Christmas had not been marked as an important holiday. The newcomers—with their stoellen, their Christmas trees, ornaments, and candlelight, and always their music—changed all that. Even in the old country where a boy might walk twelve miles for a piece of white bread, the shortening, fruit, and flour were set aside for weeks beforehand in readiness for the holiday bread whose preparation was entrusted to the community baker. In the Germans' adopted country, where cream and butter, meat, and dried fruits were all more plentiful, Christmas could be fittingly celebrated. During the dark winter afternoon, women would sit around embroidered tablecloths with their knitting and fancywork, sipping strong coffee and nibbling at ring cakes, *Streuselkuchen*, cheesecake, and anise cookies baked long before and set aside to mellow for the occasion.[24] Sometimes bread and butter and thinly sliced ham would be served, and there would be a bowl of whipped cream for the coffee. They would linger, urged by the hostess or her maid, until it was nearly time for the light seven o'clock supper at home, with a Herman or Otto or Fritz dismayed that no one was there to put it on the table.

In well-to-do German households such as the Dolge's, Christmas was a ritual. In the center of the high double parlor there rose a fir tree decorated with glass balls, icicles, elves, and angels, all wrought with marvelous care and brought over from Germany. Sometimes the tree stayed up, with a sheet underneath to catch the needles, until Easter. The children were urged to play with their intricate new toys, their games, blocks and miniature vehicles in the room assigned to them, while the grownups drank coffee, rock crystal brandy, or anisette and talked and sang "O Tannenbaum" and other holiday favorites. The village was becoming a marvellously good place to live, full of lieder and love.

One of Alfred Dolge's last Christmas cards showed him seated at a piano. He had made a good life. He had also made enemies, as any reformer and innovator is bound to do. And he had his worries. But for as long as he could, he kept those to himself.

CHAPTER 5

HINTS OF TROUBLE

Not all the German immigrants were blessed with Dolge's oak leaf on the shoulder stamina. For one of his employees, the experience of beginning over in the New World ended in tragedy.

Anna Schroeder remembered him well. "Fritz Kloetzler was a skilled shoemaker, very proud of his trade. He settled in Dolgeville and brought his family over. At that time Alfred Dolge could not finance the making of stock; consequently the shoe department was closed every winter for a number of years. As he had a large lumber interest in the North Country and the lumber was brought to Dolgeville from the sawmills every winter, he gave the unemployed married men a chance to earn a living temporarily by piling lumber. Kloetzler was offered a job, but he refused it. He was very proud, and piling lumber was coming down the social ladder for a skilled shoemaker. (Such a man could judge leather, take measurements, make his own patterns, and complete a pair of shoes.)

"As he had much time on his hands in winter, he read a lot and did a great deal of thinking and brooding. He became an atheist and some said an anarchist. His wife's health was failing, and she became discouraged for they had no relatives in this country. There were four children, ranging from three to eleven years. Finally they became desperate and decided to end their lives and take the children with them so as not to leave them orphans in what they felt was a cold and unjust world.

"The furniture was sold gradually to buy food, and the children were told that they were moving to Boston and would have a better home there. When all plans were completed, Kloetzler sent a long letter to a German newspaper in New York City and another one to Alfred Dolge at his New York office, denouncing the world and everything in it, and ending with the words that by the time these lines reached him, Kloetzler and his family would not be with the living.

"Alfred Dolge immediately telephoned to the office in Dolgeville and asked two men to go to Kloetzler's home, find out what was the matter, and see that they had everything they needed. He would talk to Kloetzler himself when he came over the weekend.

"When the men went there, they found a very bare house. Kloetzer and his wife had just given the smaller children some black coffee, which no doubt contained poison. The father was carrying the youngest child in his arms as it was whimpering. He looked desperate and refused all offers of help, saying they would soon be leaving and had all they needed for the trip.

"The men, realizing that all was not well, left to get more help and bring the police along. When they returned some time later, the house was in complete darkness except for the light from a small lamp at the head of the stairs, which lighted the way to a bedroom. There on three mattresses lay the suicide and his entire family. With the help of his wife he had been able to do it all very quickly. The younger children had died of poison and the rest had slashed throats. He had slashed his wrists to hasten death. A large satchel in the room was found to contain clothing for the entire family for burial.

"For the sake of the children the family was given a Christian burial on the following Sunday afternoon from the home. The Methodist minister had charge of the service, and a quartet from the same church sang several hymns. The family was buried in one large grave in the Dolgeville cemetery."[1]

Fritz Kloetzler had been an educated man, unlike some of the established members of the community whom Dolge was to describe as "barely able to write their names." But Dolge did not for a moment draw the conclusion that reading, and brooding over what he had read, whether or not it had led to Kloetzler's suicide, was a thing to be condemned. An educated man himself, Dolge believed in universal education as deeply as he believed in anything. When he arrived in the town, there had been a one-room primary school and nothing more. Some of the well-to-do residents sent their children to Fairfield Academy, just over the hill from Brockett's Bridge; the Lambersons—Roy, Dora, and Jennie—Charlie and Dan Sullivan, Dr. Strobel, Dr. W.H. Petrie, and George Arnold had all been educated there. A very few went to private schools farther away. For the rest of the village, high school had been out of the question. Furthermore "the number of children had increased surprisingly" which was not so surprising when one recalls those German picnics as Carl Carmer's father, a principal, observed.

The more he thought of it, the more Alfred Dolge found such a state of education intolerable. In which he chose to think of as an otherwise model community, who could abide "Man who had been brought up with no comprehension of the duties toward future generations, but who preferred ignorance and poor schools to a few shillings for taxes."[2] Once he had resolved to act on his conviction, the battle lines were drawn. In no area of life was there such clear-cut disagreement between the old Yankee settlers and the new Dutch. Members of the *Turnverein*, which had mental as well as physical improvement among its aims, enjoyed discussing local problems. Having reached the conclusion that the "largest taxpayers, who consist mostly of retired farmers, always strenuously objected to any improvement of the village if such improvement would in the least increase the taxes,"[3] also recognized that the support of American-born citizens would be needed. Therefore the first step was to form a School Society. The original nucleus was all German (including all the Dolges);[4] but before the month was out, a meeting had been held on August 30, 1886 at which men with such names as A. G. Barney and Con Sullivan were among the officers elected. Henry Dolge became the Society's first president.[5] The next step was to appoint a building committee whose members, with one exception, were natives, as representing the largest taxpayers and property owners. The one exception was Alfred Dolge himself.[6]

The minutes of their meetings record a minor digression concerning the temperance-minded local people who were ready to support "useless experiments" in saving the heathen of the South Seas but "cannot educate their own children." Otherwise they went straight to work, resolving to put up Theodore Sanford for election as trustee at the next district school meeting. He won easily.

On September 28, 1886, after a good deal of politicking in stores and other meeting places and much canvassing to get out the German vote, the meeting was held and plans worked out by Alfred Dolge were proposed. He would give the land and $1,000. Three thousand dollars more would be realized from the sale of the old schoolhouse grounds, and $6,000 would be raised through taxes. The proposal carried by a vote of 82 to 7.[7]

In all, thirteen meetings of the building committee were held. Alfred Dolge, as chairman, was present at all of them. He examined every detail—the obtaining of estimates "for stone, brick and iron," whether the window sills should be of brick or stone—and made inquiries about heaters and furnaces. A bee was held to grade the site and the cornerstone was laid with an elaborate ceremony.[8] Despite the favorable vote, Dolge soon realized that carrying out the proposal was not going to be easy.

His frustration showed itself in the first issue of a paper he called the *Scrutinizer* (January 22, 1887) which from now on would be issued annually. Tucked away among more straight-forward comment was a piece of heavy irony that perhaps had as much to do with the building of schoolhouses as with its ostensible subject:

VILLAGE ORDINANCES

The fire company is hereby disbanded, and the engine will be sold for old copper. We had no such new fangled institutions fifty years ago, and we live yet.

The building of new fences and sidewalks, and the repairing of sidewalks is hereby made a misdemeanor; it only encourages the girls to promenade the streets.

The burning of street lamps after 8 P.M. is hereby prohibited as a useless expense and tending to make people keep late hours.

All intended improvements (so called) have to be sanctioned by the committee on ye olden times, which sits every day.

M.U. Lish
President of the Hamlet

G.R. Umbler, Clerk
Brockett's Bridge, Jan. 1, 1887
(Was Dolgeville) 9#

In that same issue, Dolge's feelings on the subject of education were expressed more directly. "I have often wished that the entire Congress could for six months be sent away from Washington and each representative be compelled to travel through his district, stop at every single schoolhouse, and investigate what facilities the workingmen's children, especially in the country towns, have for education.

"When they strike a village like ours where we have over 350 children who ought to go to school and have only one school house that can accommodate not more than 100 children; when the principal of our school has to hire out to the farmer during harvest time, to make hay at $2 a day, because he cannot live on the scant salary allowed him; when the trustees of the school district are obliged to hire girls of 14 and 15 years, to teach our boys, because those girls are willing to teach for $3 a week, such teaching as you can expect of a mere child, because the school taxes have to be paid by the hard working farmers and the working men, who both, perhaps, have all they can do to pay the interests of mortgages on their homesteads; when they will see that you, the working men of this place had to club together to form a School Society, simply for the purpose of securing only the most necessary schooling for your children; when they see that you pay voluntarily, besides your regular school taxes from 10¢ to $1 and more each month into the treasury of that school society; when these gentlemen see all this; when they find a similar state of affairs almost everywhere, except in large cities, I have no doubt that some of them would come back to Washington with an idea that it might not be amiss to start a National School Commission; start National Teachers' Seminaries, and spend millions of dollars every year for the education of the poor men's children, and keep vigilant officers employed who will see that the children do attend the school, or the parents be properly called to account, if this has been neglected."

The forthright methods Dolge now proceeded to use were hardly democratic; many called him a dictator. Whether anything less high handed would have succeeded at the time, it would be hard to say. As chairman of the building committee, he hounded the taxpayers of the village with letters that were not diplomatic. One dated May 22, 1887 read simply:

> Dear Sir: My list shows that you contributed nothing in work or money for the levelling of the school house grounds. If this is not correct please inform me at once and oblige.
>
> Yours truly,
> Alfred Dolge

By October, the pressure on delinquent contributors took the form of extortion, as a letter dated October 4, 1887 makes clear:

> Dear Sir:
> The Building Committee of this District has resolved to invite the inhabitants to take part in a bee for levelling the school house grounds on October 6 and 7, under the supervision of Mr. Peter J. Dunckel, and instructed me to send out the invitations. I am informed that you did not take part in the bee we had this spring, and as you are an inhabitant and consequently directly interested in the public enterprises, I have no doubt but that this direct appeal will induce you either to send a

team, if you have one, or pay according to your means for hiring teams. It costs $3.00 a day per team, and the committee thinks that each property owner should *at least* send a team for one day or pay $3.00. However we will take whatever you see fit to pay, no matter how small the amount. I beg to state that a little book will be published in time, on the history of this village, and the names of those with the amounts subscribed will be printed in that book, also of those who decline to take part in the bee. If you cannot send a team or man to work, will you kindly send your subscription before October 5th to my office and very much oblige.

Yours truly,
Alfred Dolge

On October 15, 1887—a bright blue autumn day—the new building was opened and dedicated with the usual German fanfare: flags and bands, many speeches, citizens in carriages, and a huge crowd. The Dolges opened their house on Main Street to entertain the out-of-town guests.

Meanwhile, the harassment of the delinquents continued. A letter to one of them, dated November 8, 1887, read:

Dear Sir:

I am informed that you did not contribute anything, either in cash or labor, towards grading of the School-house lot. If this is correct, I beg to inform you that there still is a balance of over $30.00 to be paid by voluntary contribution, and that I am ready to accept whatever you see fit to give, at my office until December 1st. If you have not paid on that day, I will take it for granted that you do not intend paying anything.

If the above information is not correct, please state in writing, how much you have paid and to whom, as I am very anxious to have the list correct in every particular.

Very truly yours,
Alfred Dolge

The threat to publish a list of noncontributors, along with those who had contributed either more or less than their share in the assessment, had not been an idle one either. In 1888 a nicely bound book appeared under the title, *The First Union Free School of Dolgeville, New York.*

With strict fairness, Alfred Dolge's name appeared in the list of those who had thus far contributed less than their share.[10]

Among the records of the Dolgeville School Board is a telegram from Dolge in New York City: "Can't make the meeting on the Central." One can picture his fury as he dashed off that message—or presiding, with eyes narrowed, a cigar clamped firmly between his teeth (one of 26 a day), over the series of meetings that made the new school building an eventual reality. He had served as president of the Board since the beginning. By October 10, it seemed as though he had had enough. A letter he wrote to the Board on that date, dashed off without correction and signed with such vehemence that it blotted where the pen dug in, tells something of the story:

> When I accepted the office as a member of your board I done so in the hope of being able to promote the interest of our village. I found, however, that my ideas regarding schools and their management are so utterly and uncompromisingly at variance with those of the majority of your board, that my further presence in your meetings can not produce any good results.
>
> The actions taken by the board at the meetings of Sept. 12 and Oct. 3, are such that I cannot—conscientious of the serious and grave responsibilities which the office carries with it, even apparently sanction them, or give my silent consent.
>
> I therefore beg to tender my resignation as President and member of your board.
>
> Respectfully
> Alfred Dolge

Behind this letter lay what Dolge wrote of in 1890 as "the most bitter fight I ever had to go through." A communication from the School Society had asked that German be taught in the school. This was read to the Board, and a reply was sent back to the effect that "steps had already been taken that no foreign language should be taught compulsory."

According to the records of the Board, at a meeting on November 7 there was a motion by J. B. Koetteritz that a committee of two be appointed to "sit on Alfred Dolge and induce him to stay on the Board." The committee of two, consisting of A. G. Barney and H. Faville, reported back their belief that "if we refuse to accept his resignation he will continue."[11] There was a unanimous vote not to accept it, and at the next meeting Alfred Dolge was back, fighting more uphill battles.

The next of these had to do with physical education. There was a gymnasium in the basement of the new school, and Dolge proposed that all teachers be instructed to give physical exercises to the children during the first ten minutes each morning. The motion succeeded; another to having singing taught in the school, failed for the time being. Dolge then declared that he "had planned to give the district a grand piano and hire a music teacher at his own expense." (He eventually paid most of the $18,000 that the school cost.)

The sorest point was still the resentment toward himself as an innovator and a German. He had heard the principal say, "Down with the Dutch—Vote the American ticket," and was quoted later as saying that, "Certain members of the board had been very busy telling the voters that I intended to Germanize the school and possibly the whole village."[12]

That Dolge was bringing in German ideas of education there could be no doubt. His notion of cultural improvement in a rustic setting was thoroughly German, and at odds with the frugal and cautious outlook of the older inhabitants. So was the idea of kindergarten. Originating with August Froebel in Germany, it had been transplanted to the New World by Margarethe Meyer Schurz, the wife of Carl Schurz, who had opened a kindergarten for German children at Watertown, Wisconsin in 1856. By 1888 some public schools had begun adding kindergartens, but Dolgeville was the first town in New York State to offer a kindergarten free for all. It began in January 1889, in the upstairs clubhouse of one of the Dolge factories, at what is now No. 2 Factory, Elm Street, with Miss Rust as a teacher.[13] Twenty children attended that first year. It was Dolge's view that "the public school should commence with the kindergarten where the children from their 3rd year of age are under the care of an experienced teacher who carefully prepares their minds, and while apparently letting them play, develops their sense of order, cleanliness, beauty, etc. Guided by their teachers they will receive at the kindergarten an education which nine-tenths of all mothers could not possibly impart if they tried to and if their household duties permitted."[14]

A packet of intricately-woven mats from that early kindergarten attests to a training of young eyes and fingers quite different from that which prevails today.[15]

By the time the kindergarten opened, the continual disagreements between the Board of Education and the School Society had led Dolge to think of an academy, to be run according to the philosophy of education that had aroused so much opposition. He had found two boys working in his office who—he declared publicly not long after his attempted resignation from the Board—could not do the simplest sums. That outraged him; but his concern for education went much further than any question of arithmetic. His speech at the dedication of the First Union Free School made this clear:

"As a people, we have, in fact, become criminally careless as to our most sacred duty, namely, to make, by force of good education, every child a good citizen; and have lost sight of the fact that when we open our ports for all the poor and needy, we open them also to the ignorant and uneducated, who, because of their ignorance, are the easy prey of the reckless agitators and adventurers.

"The future of this great country, the inviolability of our free and liberal institutions, can be guarded only by a rising generation, which, by means of a most excellent education, will not alone keep that unruly element in check, but raise it up, elevate it, so that it will generate good and useful citizens of our great republic, citizens able to analyze and understandingly resist the false teachings of the adventurous agitators and revolutionists. Better than standing armies, better than iron which would not be consistent with the liberty-breathing spirit of our Constitution; better than laws restricting emigration, which we need to develop our great South and West; better than anything that our law-makers can devise, will be the education of our rising generation and the building of schoolhouses, even in the remotest corners of our great country; for then the theorist, demagogue, or glib-tongued agitator will everywhere be confronted by audiences who have been educated to think for themselves."[16]

The opening of the kindergarten was the first of a series of moves and counter-moves by the School Society and the Board of Education. Also in January 1889, the School Society removed its support from the Union Free School and opened a school of its own. Altogether it had 79 pupils with 20 in the kindergarten and 59 in the grammar grades. In six months 108 attended. As a result the Union Free School, though so newly built, now stood almost empty. It was now that Dolge undertook to build at his own expense what was to become the Dolgeville Academy. As it neared completion, a petition to unite the two schools was circulated. A newly elected Board agreed to the School Society's terms, one of which was to retain the kindergarten. Beginning February 27, 1890, both schools were part of the Union Free District, although the Academy was privately run and for years charged tuition. The union of both schools became a fact on April 1, 1890.[17] It was approved by the Regents of the State of New York as a Union Free District in 1895.[18] The School Society contributed about $1,000 a year to its support, in addition to the amount that came from taxes. In 1895 when the Board announced its wish to end the kindergarten, the School Society withdrew its support for the school and applied the $1,000 to the kindergarten alone. Beginning in 1895, in a last tempest, the kindergarten was part of the Academy.[19] However, in 1895 the Academy was turned over finally to the Board of Education and granted high school status by the Regents.[20] Two school governing bodies had not worked well together.

The Academy building, which had been dedicated on August 30, 1890, was variously estimated to have cost anywhere from $10,000 to $20,000. In addition to space for the kindergarten, it included a public library with living quarters for the librarian as well as a janitor. Among the innovations was a form of air conditioning: "The cold air as taken from the outside is carried down to the basement floor and from thence directly under the furnace. This air is kept moist by a stream of running water that comes from a spring a short way distant and flows directly through the air shaft."[21] Electric lights, electric bells, and fire escapes were further up-to-date features. The state Superintendent of Education, Andrew S. Draper, came to speak at the dedication. "It is doubtful," he said, "if there is another village in the State of New York which has so much money invested in school property as has Dolgeville."[22] He commented as well on the German respect for trained teachers, and declared that American school teachers ought to be as carefully trained as candidates for the professions of divinity, medicine, and law.

It was clear that Draper's ideas closely paralleled those of Alfred Dolge, who once again spoke of his ideas on education: "The public school is the field where the seed of a belief in religious liberty, of tolerance, of freedom of thought, must be sown." He envisioned a public school "in which the child of the free thinker can sit next to the child of the orthodox Christian or Hebrew . . . . Only with the aid of such public schools," he declared, "can we . . . fulfill what the scientists tell us is our destiny: the production of a race distinguished above all others the world has yet seen for the freedom of its institutions, its love of liberty, its progress in the arts and sciences, and its broad humanitarianism."[23]

The first class formed in 1897 to graduate from the Academy had ten members: Anna Youker, Phoebe Spencer, Gaie Barney, Ben Sullivan, Harry White, Edward M. Brown, George Kneaskern, and Aaron Wagner. By 1899, when they received their diplomas, Alfred Dolge would no longer be present to congratulate them.

Will Schuchardt.

OTTO VOIGT

PRINCIPAL STYLES

OF THE

ALFRED DOLGE FELT SHOES,

DANIEL GREEN & CO.,

SOLE AGENTS,

FOR DESCRIPTION AND PRICE, SEE CATALOGUE.

UTICA, N. Y.

DOLGEVILLE, N. Y.
MAY 28 1887

No. 3.

No. 4.

No. 5.

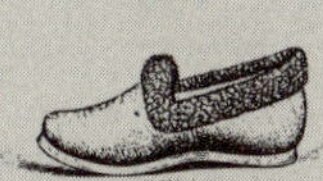

No. 11.

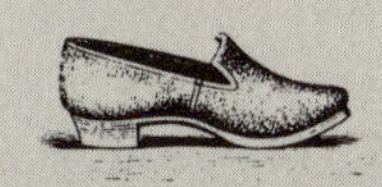

No. 14.

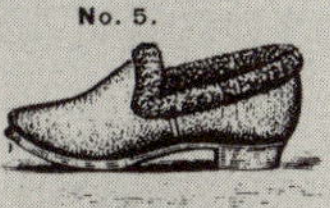

No. 15.

No. 17.

No. 20.

No. 21.

No. 24.

No. 26.

No. 28.

No. 29.

No. 35.

No. 40.

Description of Infants' Polish, No. 38,

Made from Felt [illegible] inch thick, making them soft and warm. Also used as overshoes for infants and will fit nicely, and are the only overshoe made for infants.

No. 38.

COLORS.--Dark Blue, Red, Drab and Black.

LADIES' CARRIAGE BOOT.

These are introduced to wear over slippers or shoes by Ladies', driving or attending parties, to protect the ankles and feet.

COLOR.—Dark Blue.

Ladies' Carriage Boot.

RUBBER BOOT SLIPPER are of the same style and appearance as No. 40.

Will furnish any of these CUTS to parties making a specialty of our goods.

Leading styles of Dolge's felt shoes in 1887.

...PATENT HAIR FELT...

Of — **ALFRED DOLGE & SON.**

The Patent Consists of the INNOVATION of...

Interfelting the Finest White or Blue Hair with the... Highest Grades of Wool

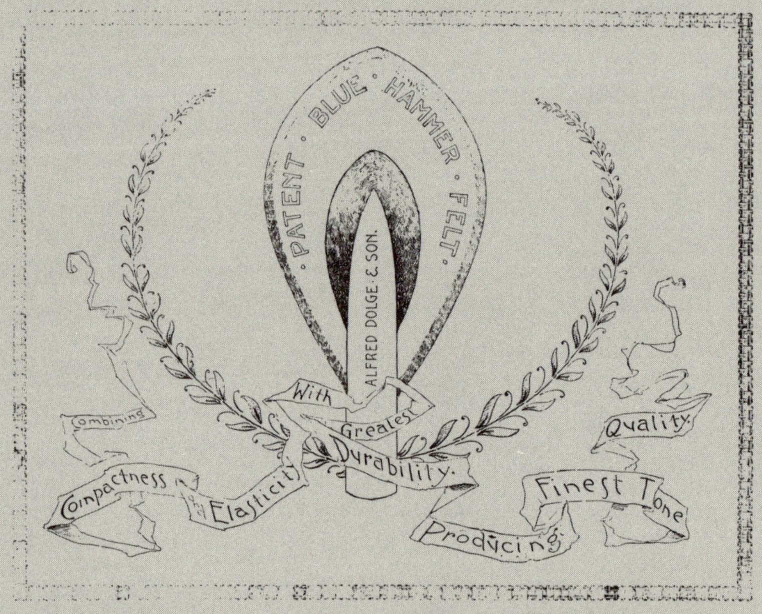

Which Produces a Combination of..... Compactness and Elasticity *with* Greatest Durability, *and thereby producing*

Finest Tone Quality in Piano Hammers *and in*
Damper, Wedge and Muffler Felts, THUS WITH THE FINE, EVEN SURFACE THE VIBRATION OF STRINGS IS PREVENTED THEREFORE ARE THE PERFECTION AS MUTES IN....

"Blue or White Hair Felts."

Piano hammer felt advertisement from *The Presto Yearbook*, 1896.

Strings masthead, Vol. I, No. 1, April 1894. Claiming to be "tuned to the trade," this first issue promised "no twaddle," but instead, "the clear ring of the Anvil Chorus of the music tradesmen beating out their living with the hammer of business."

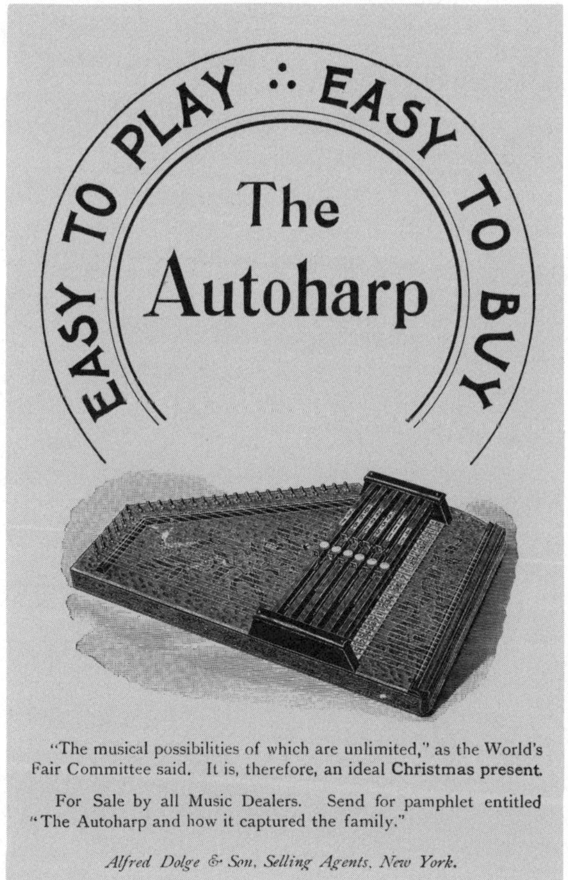

Autoharp advertisement from *Strings*, November 1894.

Wine list for a banquet, December 31, 1889.

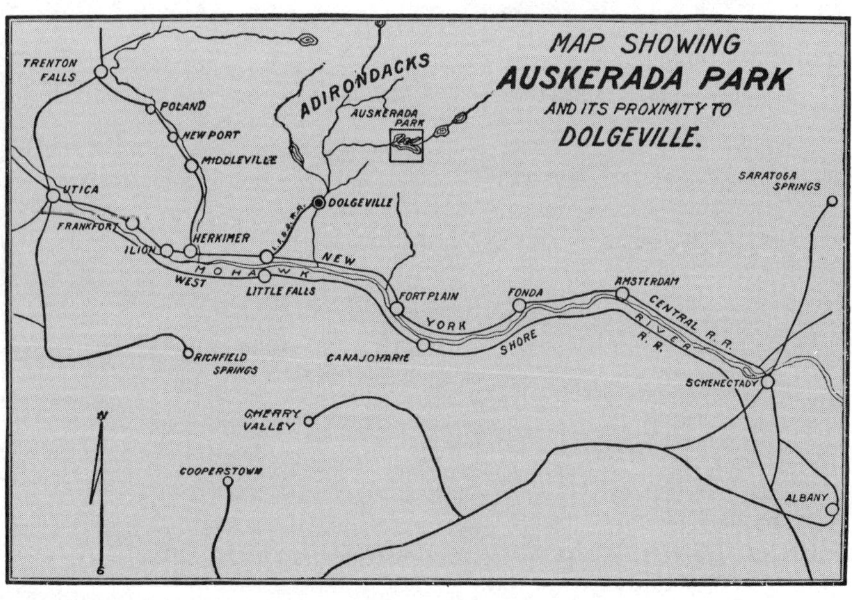

Map from the Auskerada Park prospectus.

THE AUTOHARP.

Easy to Play — Easy to Buy

Style 4--$15.00

All Music Dealers sell this style, or we will send it prepaid upon receipt of price. with instructions, picks, music, etc.

THE more one sees and hears the AUTOHARP, the more is its charm and beauty recognized. It embodies all the desirable features and essential requirements of a musical instrument. Anyone can learn to play it. Prices to suit all purses, $4.00, $5.00, $7.50, $10.00 and up to $150.00. Write for illustrated story and catalogue.

ALFRED DOLGE & SON,
Dept. 2, Dolge Building, New York City.

Autoharp Style 4 is deservedly one of the most popular. At a medium price it offers the player a wide scope by reason of the judicious grouping of the chords which permit most beautiful modulations. The finish of this Autoharp is very handsome, the sides and bottom are of imitation ebony and rosewood highly polished. The bars and supports are ebonized and the top finished in natural color California Redwood.

"Easy to play—Easy to buy." Autoharp advertisement from souvenir program of the November 1897 Dolgeville Fair and Bazaar.

CHAPTER 6

THE INVESTMENTS

By 1890 the felt and molding industries were employing many of the 1,500 new settlers in Dolgeville. Two hundred more shoemakers were needed. There was a piano factory, a woolen factory, and a wire factory. The pension plan was operating. Things looked good. As the *Dolgeville Herald* declared in September of that year, "Never in the history of this village was there a time when the sky of prosperity surrounding us assumed a brighter hue." It was in that year that Alfred Dolge's long cherished dream of a railroad from Dolgeville to Little Falls at last began to take shape.

As long ago as 1882, Dolge had subscribed $10,000 toward the project—only to see the Little Falls business men who had made surveys give up their plans. The reason, according to Dolge, had been that "a land speculation which was the real motive for building the railroad could not be carried out as planned."[1] But with the factories prospering as they now were, the gamble of a railroad that would replace the fifty teams required to transport the 4,000 pounds of lumber and again of other merchandise to Little Falls seemed justified. The great horse barn on Dolge Avenue that had housed the teams could then be converted into a factory for the growing felt shoe business.

Again in Dolge's own words, "The building of the road was an engineering feat of no small proportions. There is a steep wall of rock on the northern side of the [New York] Central tracks at Little Falls, and to reach the table lands above it was necessary to climb that wall of rock. The road bed was hewn from a ledge of solid stone for a distance of nearly three miles from the southern terminus. The road crosses a number of ravines, and cuts through some very formidable hills. The bridges and cuts are considered remarkable for a road of its length, one cut being 500 feet long and 40 feet deep. The bridges are of iron, and the road bed is ballasted with rock."[2]

The building took two years rather than the estimated six months.

Two contractors failed in the process, and in the end the cost came to $575,000 (according to Dolge in his *History of a Crime*) rather than the originally estimated $230,000. But Alfred Dolge persisted, watching the debts mount and shouldering them one by one. Since 1882, when the original surveys were made, he had come to rely on the advice of two men who were prominent in Little Falls: George Anson Hardin, a judge of the State Supreme Court and a director of the National Herkimer County Bank and Schuyler Ingham, a businessman whose quickness and flair Dolge found attractive.[3] Both had been gratefully acknowledged as contributors to the campaign of the School Society in 1886. Ingham, whose main residence was not with his family but in a New York hotel, was soon representing Dolge's interests there and in Washington, where he lobbied in support of the preferential tariff. With Judge Hardin, Dolge called on leading businessmen of Little Falls in an effort to raise a bond issue of $250,000 to finance the railroad.[4] Dolge himself took a loan of $50,000 from the Herkimer bank, and another for the same amount from the American Exchange Bank of New York. In 1891, after the second contractor failed, a group of Wall Street bankers organized to finance the work that remained to be done. Dolge had lost $180,000 before the railroad went into operation.

Much of the work was done by laborers of Italian extraction, who were remembered by the local people as trudging to their work carrying long loaves of bread for lunch. One man, DeWitt Ward, remembered the laying of the rails in 1892. "This was done by a gang of Negroes from the South," he said. "They worked very harmoniously, and it was interesting to hear them sing as they placed the rails into position."

During those two years, Dolge had other worries besides the railroad. One of these was the recurring danger of fire. As long ago as 1879 he had organized a bucket brigade, known as the Volunteer Fire Company No. 1. Even with a new hand pumper, it had not been able to prevent the loss of half the buildings along Main Street to the destructive fire of 1882. In March 1887, the Excelsior Hose Company No. 1 was formed, but that too proved insufficient to protect all the Dolge properties. In 1890 the sawmill at Leipzig burned to the ground. That loss, Dolge wrote in 1891, "following so closely after the burning of the Bungtown mill, seems to point out the advisability of concentrating the entire lumber business sawmills and all at Dolgeville."[5]

On November 28, 1892 there was still another fire. Proctor Spofford described it. He lived in a house next to his father's tin shop, where he remembers teakettles, milk cans, sections of tin roofs, sap buckets, milk pans, dippers, and stovepipes were made and sold. "We were in bed this night it happened, one or two o'clock Sunday morning. My sister woke up. She heard the crackling noise, and she hollered to my father. My father, my brothers, and I slept in a bedroom next to the store. We woke up and the glass from the window was under the bed then. He got up, and told us children to get up just as quick as we could because we had to go down in the boiler house to sound the alarm. We stepped downstairs to Ed Woods and woke them up. We saved two chairs and a feather bed. That's all we saved.

"The Klock block next door burned down, the Bowman's drug store (Dr. Getman built that) and the white house where we lived burnt to the ground. Old Dr. Barney's burned up, and the buildings across the road where the gas station is, the Barney block (they used to have a drug store) that caught afire, and the two Platt houses, they got afire, and the Barney Opera House on top of the hill, that got afire.

"Well, they got the pump engine up there and they got it down to the creek just beyond my Granddad's old house where Greenlee's store was later, and they got it down to the creek, and it wouldn't work. Well, they bothered with it and bothered with it, trying to get it going. Finally they sent to Little Falls to get their ammunition. They got the engine on the railroad. That took quite a time, and before they got it loaded on a flat car, why, they got this old pumper in order in case it was needed. So they got the fire about out."[6]

Even before the fire, the idea of damming East Canada Creek to form a reservoir had been on Dolge's list of projects. When the Dolgeville Electric Light and Power Company was formed in 1889 he was thinking ahead to the one that eventually came into being and promised that in time he would build a power plant down by High Falls that would give ten times the horsepower.[7] In January, 1895 the *Scrutinizer*'s "History of the Year" contained this item: "March 6, 1894: Alfred Dolge purchased several thousands of acres of forest lands surrounding the Canada Lakes, intending by building a dam at the outlet, to raise the water in the chain of lakes many feet, and thus form an inexhaustible reservoir from which to feed the East Canada Creek and furnish never failing power to the factories."

Dolge's energies as a firefighter never flagged. In 1896 he would organize yet another brigade, known as the Alfred Dolge Hose Company No. 1. Its members had uniforms and a horse-drawn cart, and it was they who would stand by him loyally through all the trouble that was to come.

In the meantime, on March 16, 1893, the railroad he had brought into being had been put to gala use. The occasion was the marriage of Rudolf, Alfred Dolge's eldest son, to Anita Heller-Schneller. A special train brought Rudolf's New York friends to Little Falls aboard two sleeping cars decorated with large banners reading, "This Is the Dolge Heller Bridal Party," and "Marriage Is Not a Failure." Here a number of other guests joined the party, among them Schuyler Ingham and Judge Hardin (who performed the ceremony) and their wives. The train proceeded along the scenic route to Dolgeville, overlooking the Mohawk Valley and the gorge of the East Canada Creek, passing through the two intervening stations of Ingham Mills and High Falls Park. At Dolgeville, sleighs met the train and transported the party to Alfred Dolge's house. Originally the ceremony was to have been performed at the Academy; but then, according to the account in the *Dolgeville Herald* a few days later, "Mr. Alfred Dolge who arrived in Dolgeville on Friday at midday decided that was too small." Instead, the marriage took place in the Turners' old clubhouse on Elm Street which was in the process of being turned into a factory for what was to be the Autoharp Company. "How the place, which was full of lumber, dirt, and dust on Friday at 2:00 P.M. was in twenty-four hours turned into a handsomely decorated and brilliantly lighted hall is known only to Mr. Dolge himself. But it was done and the building roofed over, retiring and dressing rooms and kitchens built, flowers and plants distributed . . . . The decorations consisted of American and German flags and rich hangings set off with evergreens and flowers."

Judge Hardin conducted the ceremony before a bower of flowers and plants. "Marriage," he told the gathering, "is the loveliest contract known to human beings."

Alfred Dolge offered these words of advice: "Why does a man work? To help those he loves. Be as happy as I and my wife have been for twenty-five years."

Christian Dolge, by now a venerable figure quite different from the revolutionary firebrand of 1848, spoke at length. "I stand before you an old oak," he began. "A mother of old once said: 'Do you wish your husband to be your servant, you must be his handmaid and if you are his handmaid he will be your slave.' My Anita: you have a mother-in-law who will be your stay in trouble and sorrow. If you are in trouble go to her. She has been through a school as not one in a thousand have and for that very reason she is to be envied. It is given but to few young wives to have such a mother-in-law. My dear Rudolf: you are the crown prince of

Dolgeville . . . I believe that you will be the same good father to your children as your father was to his children . . . . Your marriage is different from your father's. When he married he did so very quietly, and sent unstamped notices of the event to us all in Germany, on which we had to pay double postage . . . . Like your father you have married very young . . . .

"You will find you want to make all men happy," the old man continued, "but like him you will find you cannot. In all your life do not forget that in the smallest, humblest man there is the 'dignity of man.' Do not forget that in the poorest workman in your factory may be the power of a great minister of state and that he cannot express this power because his hands are bound. Therefore in all things be just! And most of all be careful, be considerate of the least of those with whom you have to do. Let it be with you 'man to man.' "[8]

Rudolf's bride was a young girl of German parentage, who had been born in Bogota, Colombia and later adopted by a wealthy aunt. She had traveled for a while with Anna Dolge in Germany, and it was thus that Rudolf met her. His parents' great admiration for the explorer and naturalist Alexander von Humboldt had led to his own interest in South America. Before settling in Dolgeville, Rudolf's uncle, Henry Dolge, had migrated to Venezuela. Not many years later, Rudolf himself would go there. In the meantime, he had been made his father's partner, and would be put in charge of the autoharp factory.

The bride wore "a white satin dress elaborately trimmed with fine point lace. She had a veil of silk tulle fastened to her hair with orange blossoms. She carried a bouquet of bride's roses and lilies of the valley. She wore no jewelry.

"Mrs. Alfred Dolge wore a charming costume of brown faille and velvet, ornaments—diamonds and pearls. Bouquet of pale yellow roses." Descriptions of six bridesmaids' dresses and the gowns of twenty-eight guests followed. Mrs. S. R. Ingham and Mrs. George Hardin were among them.

The festive mood of that March wedding day was not to last. In April, a financial panic swept across the nation. The high hopes Alfred Dolge had had of McKinley's protectionist tariff were not fulfilled. Bankruptcies were common. Following Alfred Dolge's losses on the railroad, the destruction of the new woolen mill managed by Hugo Dolge came as one more blow—an outlay of $30,000 gone up in smoke. There had been a "sharp flash of lightning and an awful clap of thunder . . . at the same instant and in a few minutes the glare of fire showed up in the direction of the woolen mill. It was entirely consumed . . ." on June 17, 1894.[9] The mill was reopened at Dryden, near Ithaca, where its success continued to rise and fall with the business in Dolgeville, which gave notes to cover its indebtedness.

The building of the new Turnhall had cost Dolge $40,000. He had recently invested $40,000 more in a large farm belonging to Phillip Helmer, which was being graded and laid out into residential lots. The project would be profitable eventually, no doubt; but now it added to the burden of Dolge's indebtedness—$400,000 in non-profit-bearing property, with $24,000 annual interest.[10]

The finances of the country were inevitably reflected in Dolgeville. Though he was still determined not to be forced to the wall as so many had been, in the winter of 1893–94 Alfred Dolge was obliged for the first time to shut down his factories for want of orders. They stayed closed for three months. On January 27, 1894, the occasion of what in better times would have been the annual banquet, he reported to his employees as they sat around empty tables. The $500 that the banquet would have cost was given instead to alleviate the needs of the working men; however, only $100 of it had to be used, and eventually the remainder went to the School Society.

In a long speech, Dolge spoke of conditions throughout the country: "Dolgeville knows as yet nothing of soup houses. Most of you own your own homes and when the factories are closed we have saved enough to carry you through the winter without asking alms of anybody." He went on to blame Free Trade for the situation, but ended on a note of optimism: industry, he pointed out, had brought the assessed total worth of Dolgeville from $30,000 to over $1,200,000.

A year later, at the banquet on January 31, 1895, Dolge was describing the success of his insurance and pension plan; he had paid $31,367.75 into the pension fund, and the premiums he had paid on policies for his employees now totaled $34,595.27. He had even paid funds into banks to protect employees who had been rejected by insurance companies. After twenty years of trying to work out his own solution to the problem of financial insecurity, he believed he had found one that worked. Eight of his employees were now retired and were living on their share of the pension fund. He was now urging nationalization of his system, and especially he recommended it to the railroads. "A contribution of one percent of the amount of wages earned, paid by the employer annually into a National Insurance Fund would be ample," he declared.[11]

He was traveling widely now, speaking in Chicago to the Music Trade Association, in New York to the Piano Manufacturers' Association on his pet topics—profit-sharing, education, and protectionism. In December 1895 an *Industrial Edition* of the Little Falls *Journal and Courier* devoted twenty-six pages to Dolgeville. It summarized the history of the town and its industries, with emphasis on Dolge as a pioneer in the manufacture of piano felt. Space was given to the Autoharp Company, the Brambach Piano Company, and the other industries, as well as to the Electric Light and Power Company, the *Dolgeville Herald*, and the purchase of the Canada Lakes. Although a hundred houses had been built every year, it was noted, there was not a vacant house in the village. The pension system Dolge had instituted was described and the average wages were reported to be higher than in any similar factories in the United States or Europe. In an approving summary, the paper suggested that Dolgeville had a "still more brilliant prospect"—of growth, perhaps, to a community of at least 30,000 inhabitants.[12]

The depression had been weathered, or so it seemed. Or was the talk of progress anything more than whistling to keep up courage?

CHAPTER 7
CALAMITY

The industries had survived the panic of 1893 and come through at very little cost for welfare for the men. In 1894 Dolge divested himself of the felt shoe manufacturing, and the Daniel Green Company took over. It was incorporated with $300,000 capital and brought in much needed funding to the Dolge industries. According to the January 26, 1895 *Scrutinizer*, Daniel Green moved to the converted stables on Dolge Ave. Dolge remained on its Board of Directors. In 1896 he was only too happy to turn over the woodworking end of the business to Julius Breckwoldt, who had been with the firm since 1877 and knew the manufacture of sounding boards, moldings, and cases thoroughly.

At the end of 1896 the partnership of Alfred Dolge and Son was dissolved. Rudolf had long been in poor health; in 1895, an insurance company would have refused him a life insurance policy except that Rudolf's father "had heavy investments in the company, so they agreed on a policy of $1,000." The doctor who gave him a medical examination had told him he had not more than six months to live.[1] Fortunately he was mistaken. But by January 1897, Rudolf had decided to leave for Venezuela to begin a new life as manager of a warehouse for the National Association of Manufacturers. That his health was not the only reason for his departure was later to be revealed.

In 1897 the *Dolgeville Republican* began to supplement the *Herald* in its accounts of daily happenings. In 1897, too, the dam had been built at Stewart's Landing and construction of the electric power station at High Falls was begun. Dedicated on January 15, 1898, with a typically German ceremony, it would furnish power to Little Falls. Stores and households were decorated with bunting, flags, and streamers to welcome Lieutenant Governor Timothy L. Woodruff, who was to set the machinery in operation. Guests arrived by rail in a gloomy drizzle, to be met by the town's cornet band and driven in sleighs to hotels and then to the Dolge mansion for lunch.

"At precisely 6:15 o'clock," according to a report in the *Dolgeville Republican* for February 10, 1898, the Lieutenant Governor turned the starting wheel. "As the new light shone forth three hearty cheers were given for the High Falls electric plant, and three more with the tiger for Alfred Dolge . . . and there followed a scene of handshaking and jubilant congratulations. At the Turnhall the high ceiling was a blaze of vari-colored electric light, the principal design consisted of red, white and blue incandescent lamps in the form of a large star." There were eleven banquet tables in this largest and best appointed theater in Herkimer County. A total of 237 guests were served *truité saumonee, filet de boeuf à la godard*, and *biscuit tortoni.*[2] The Excelsior Orchestra played, almost hidden behind a bank of ferns, palms, and calla lillies in bloom. There was much light conversation and laughter.

In the words of Attorney General Hancock, on that day, "Dolgeville is perhaps the best known village of the state. The gentleman who had been to a great extent a leader in your enterprise has carved out for himself fame and fortune." The Hon. James Arkell, went further in his praise of Alfred Dolge: "Like Columbus, he did not create a new world. . . . He found one and changed it. . . . If he is a benefactor who makes two blades grow where one grew before, the man who harnesses the forces of nature and creates a thousand homes in the wilderness, and gives work to hundreds of willing hands, is more than a benefactor—he is a philanthropist."[3]

Exactly one month later, the battleship *Maine* blew up in Havana Harbor; 260 men were killed. On April 25, 1898, Congress voted to declare war against Spain. It was all over by mid-August; but even before the fighting began, Alfred Dolge's own fortunes had met with a calamity that—in Herkimer County—eclipsed the news from Washington.

According to the Feb. 10, 1898 *Dolgeville Republican* Dolge had an aggregate payroll of $10,000 to be met every week. Money was tight. All the industries in Dolgeville were Alfred Dolge. Families who went to bed happy and unsuspecting on the evening of April 10, 1898 learned before the following day's end that something had gone wrong.

Mrs. Anna Schoeder saw it all happening. "In the spring of 1898 I was working in the hammer shop in the stone building, wiring piano hammers. Toward the end of March, rumors were being circulated that all was not well with Alfred Dolge's finances. Then on April 9 and 10 the Dolgeville Railroad was carrying freight, namely wool, to Little Falls, all night; when out-of-town people were seen in the office, among them Judge Hardin and Schuyler Ingham of Little Falls, we began to ask our foreman what was the matter. He could not tell us anything. Then we asked Dan Sullivan, whose brother Charles was superintendent of the Dolgeville railroad, if he could find out something and were told, 'Charles is not talking!'

"On April 11 everyone in the factory was sure something was very wrong. The conferences behind locked doors, the anxious faces in the office were of deep concern to us all. Finally, at 5 o'clock that afternoon, one of the foremen called us together and told us to finish the work we had started, to hand in our time and to take home whatever belonged to us. He said, 'Alfred Dolge has failed, and we don't know when or if the factory will run again.'

"Now we knew. In the meantime, some of the men had gone out at two o'clock. They belonged to our local band, which was having a dance that night for new uniforms they needed. They had gone home to change and get their instruments and parade the streets as a way of advertising. As always when Dolge was in town and there was a parade, he was serenaded in front of his home. He had always greeted them and seemed very pleased and passed around a box of cigars. This time he came out with tears in his eyes and said, 'Boys, I didn't think you would do this to me.' The band men were puzzled and asked what was wrong. They had always serenaded him when they had a parade. Now he told them that he had just announced his failure. You can imagine how badly the men felt that they did not know before.

"After this every factory in Dolgeville closed its doors. It was not till September of that year, after Schuyler Ingham was made the Receiver, that the wheels began to turn again. There is no need to tell you that it was an anxious summer for all."[4]

On May 5, 1898 a meeting of creditors had been called at Ingham's hotel in Little Falls. A. M. Mills, who had been appointed receiver, read off a statement of assets and liabilities prepared under Ingham's direction. A mortgage on the Dolge factories had been foreclosed, and in due course the property was sold at auction. By September 10, the felt company was reorganized with Schuyler Ingham at its head.

Although Dolge had been aware for some time of feeling against him, the first open rumblings had come on March 21, 1898, when he presided at a meeting of the Village Board, of which he had long been president almost as a matter of course. Alderman White had moved to nominate Edward A. Brown for the office of Village Attorney. Three other members of the board now declined to second the nomination.

Dolge had looked up in surprise. All the members remained "dumb as clams," and the "silence was painful" as he asked whether he had heard a seconding of the nomination. As the evening's business moved on to the payment of bills, one from the Dolgeville Herald Publishing Company was presented for payment. Al Wait questioned Dolge's interest, saying there was a law that a public officer could not audit bills of a corporation in which he had an interest.

Dolge said, "I am not a stockholder, but they owe me money." Then he added. "I am a stockholder in the Dolgeville Electric Light and Power Company"—and without further hesitation he resigned as President of the Village Board. Later he was to declare that from the day he bought the tannery he had "toiled for and thought of nothing but the welfare of Dolgeville."[5]

Other Utopian societies had been attempted, but none of them had been quite like what he had proposed. In general, they had been based on communal ownership. Dolge had believed that what was shared should first be earned. Now his experiment was coming to an end.

Why did he fail?

Under the bald facts of the failure ran a complicated story of financial maneuverings. The situation had required more and more desperate measures. In much of his financing Dolge had depended upon the advice of two old friends.

Judge George Anson Hardin who had performed Rudolf's wedding had known Dolge since 1882 when the railroad to Little Falls was first proposed. He appeared to be an able and distinguished member of the bar who never shirked his duty, who was a New York State Supreme Court Judge for twenty-seven consecutive years and who found the time to edit an extremely good Hardin's *History of Herkimer County* (1893). It relied heavily on Benton's earlier history and on the work of Frank H. Willard, giving Hardin much credit for others work.

According to Nelson Greene's biography in the *History of the Mohawk Valley, Gateway to the West* Hardin was prominent in community affairs, a member of the citizens' committee which planned the waterworks system of Little Falls, and for more than fifty years a director of the National Herkimer County Bank. He had graduated from Union College and held court in New York City during the prosecutions of the Tweed Gang and had participated in their decisions. He was an educated man and a man of the world, the type Dolge liked best.

In 1882 when the railroad was first proposed Hardin was 50 years old, a resident of Little Falls with many state political and business connections. His ancestry and that of his wife was completely English from early New England immigrants.

Schuyler Ingham who was also an honored guest at Rudolf and Anita's wedding had come to know Alfred Dolge through Judge Hardin in 1882. He had been a clerk in the National Herkimer County Bank, manager of a bank in Iowa, and later represented the Dolge interests in Washington promoting the preferential tariff. He was from the Middle West and claimed to own a large hotel, The Kirkwood, in Des Moines, Iowa. Evidently he was attractive to Dolge for his plausibility and quick mind.[6]

Why did he fail? Why did he fail? Why did he fail?

During the months that followed, newspapers that had lauded him only a few weeks before now carried headlines that read: "A Fool or a Knave! Fraud is Charged! Caught in His Own Trap!" Rumors flew about the village. It was said that Dolge received only Ingham and Hardin and a few business men in his home. It was known that he could not cross the bridge from Fulton to Herkimer County without the prospect of being seized and held for a criminal trial because of the wool he had shipped out. Papers were served; the proceedings dragged on and on while attorneys examined his accounts. In the great quiet house, Anna Dolge saw no one. It was as though she had turned her face to the wall.

In June, an action was brought charging fraud on the part of Alfred Dolge, his son Rudolf, and the two banks—American Exchange in New York and Herkimer County in Little Falls—that held a mortgage on the factory property in Dolgeville. By September the factories were running again, but it was not until the following year that the story began to emerge, in testimony taken at the office of the Hon. A. M. Mills in Little Falls on February 20, 1899, and was reported in the *Dolgeville Herald* for April 27 of the same year.

Schuyler Ingham told his version of the story, tracing his relations with Dolge as an advisor on the building of the railroad. His concern about Dolge's financial affairs dated to the spring of 1893, when, he said, "Mr. Dolge became quite apprehensive about the amount of paper he had out, and that had been sold through brokers and was afloat on the market." One day when Ingham visited Dolge's store in New York, he had been given to understand, "without indicating the amount, that he had quite a large amount outstanding and wanted to know what I thought would be the best way of providing against it. After I got downtown, I asked myself the question as to whether or not it might not be a duty I owed to the man and especially to the bank, in which I was an officer, to go back to the store and have a very frank talk with him. I told him quite frankly that if he had had a large amount of paper floating I thought the only way in the world for him to act with any degree of safety would be to procure a permanent loan of at least $150,000 or $200,000. . . . The books were sent over to his house, and I went there, and we remained there until quite late. . . . I went down next day and laid the matter before Mr. Clark of the American Exchange National Bank, whom I knew very well, knowing that Mr. Dolge kept an account there and that they already had some paper there . . . I told Mr. Clark that if the people up in the country and the Bank of Metropolis and his bank would each give him $50,000 apiece, that in my judgement it would put him in a shape that he could go through all right. . . . At that time it was understood that Mr. Dolge should give some security for the money that was to be raised . . . I knew very little about it. . . . They told me afterwards that Mr. Dolge was to give a mortgage on the property up there and was to make a bond to each party for $100,000 and that was to cover the money that had been advanced and that would be advanced. . . . So far as the subsequent funds and the drawing up of the mortgage, etc., were concerned, that was left to and arranged between Mr. Clark and Judge Hardin."

In answer to a question from the attorney George Ward, who conducted the hearing, Ingham added that "so far as Dolge's solvency was concerned, it was not regarded as a serious thing but only as an emergency, in case of his death or a fire they could fall back on the insurance.

"And during that time," Ward later inquired, "you had several conversations with Kernan Bros. and Quin?" (Dolge's attorneys.)

"Oh, no," was Ingham's reply—"just dropping in occasionally and asking them some questions that I wanted to know particularly."

Asked whether there had been discussion of the possibility of making a valid assignment for the benefit of Alfred Dolge and Son, Ingham declined to reply. Ward: "Was anything ever said about the difficulty of bringing the property into the hands of the court on account of the absence of Rudolf in South America?"

Ingham: "No, sir." What had been discussed "was only a mere matter when these questions came up as to what protection a man could have, just mainly for the purpose of informing myself on the subject. I was only trying to inform myself legally as to what a person could do."

The testimony went on and on. It was not until March 1898, Ingham said, that he found Dolge's situation to be a real crisis. By April 8 he had finally prevaled on Dolge to go back upstate with the intention of making an assignment of his property.

Ingham: "I did telephone to Judge Hardin asking him if he could meet us in Utica on the following day, and I got an answer from him saying that he could, and I arranged with Mr. Dolge that he would be there with me and we would meet the Judge in Bagg's Hotel. This was on Saturday afternoon. . . . Mr. and Mrs. Dolge came as far as Albany with us. They were in great distress and were in one of the private rooms on the train. I was in there talking to Mrs. Dolge and Mr. Dolge and finally we all went in to dinner, and Mrs. Dolge was feeling so badly she could not eat anything, and after I had finished my dinner I went back in the observation car where they were, and while I was there Mr. Kernan (of Kernan Bros. and Quin) came up and talked with Mr. and Mrs. Dolge a little while."

As the testimony proceeded, it became evident that Rudolf Dolge had been a pivotal figure in the drama. In the summer of 1897, on a trip back to the United States, he had signed a paper giving power of attorney to a certain Robinson. On just how this had come about, Ingham was vague.

Alfred Dolge, when his turn came to testify, was more specific. In answer to a question from Ward about whether he had counseled with Ingham on financial affairs, Dolge said: "In 1893 I counseled with him, and he, then, with my cashier, made up a statement. . . . In 1896 I had several consultations with Judge Hardin and Mr. Ingham together upon the situation. "My son," Dolge went on, "was more or less present at these consultations."

Ward: "That is your son Rudolf?"

Dolge: "Yes sir."

Ward: "And in 1896 it looked for a time as though your firm would be carried down in the financial crisis?"

Dolge: "Not in my mind. Those two gentlemen tried to talk me into an assignment then."

Ward: "And they told you in substance at the time that there was no chance for you to pull through?"

"No sir, but they thought it was the wisest thing to do."

"For what reason?"

"For the creditors and myself."

"Including Judge Hardin and the National Herkimer County Bank?"

"Yes sir, of course."

"They were secured creditors at that time, were they not?"

"Yes sir."

"And none of the other creditors urged such a proceeding at that time?"

"No sir."

"How does it come," Ward asked, "that you did not take their advice at that time?"

Dolge: "I wasn't a bankrupt. I had two dollars for every dollar I owed, it was only a temporary embarrassment; I raised the money as they insisted, to bridge over the next two months until after the election—and they were in the wrong." (Dolge believed, he said, that Rudolf had fallen under the influence of the two men who had been his advisers. In direct repudiation of Ingham's testimony, Dolge declared that Rudolf "had given Mr. Robinson—or rather, Mr. Ingham had it in the beginning of May 1898, he had talked Rudolf into signing a power of attorney for Mr. Robinson or his substitute. He had empowered Mr. Robinson to substitute anybody else to commence a suit against the firm in his name to make an application for a receiver at any time Mr. Robinson saw it was necessary, and in case of the death of Alfred Dolge, Mr. Robinson was, or his substitute should at once assume control of the affairs of the firm."

Had Rudolf talked with Kernan Bros. and Quin?

Dolge: "I don't know, but when I guestioned him about the matter he said that after being a few days in New York City in May 1897, that Mr. Ingham came to him about the business and the condition I was in, the physical condition, and that the strain was so much for me that I might collapse at any day and that something ought to be done to protect the family." He had said, Dolge explained, "that because Rudolf was in South America, that somebody ought to be here who could act at once for Rudolf"—who, Dolge went on, had told his father "that he kept that paper in his pocket. Rudolf said to Mr. Ingham that he must consult me about it and Mr. Ingham said he must not do that, for if he did, that conspiracy could be successfully charged then. Rudolf kept that paper until either July or August—he isn't quite clear himself about that—he hesitated signing it but he finally did in Mr. Kernan's office."

Dolge said that the influence of Hardin and Ingham on Rudolf was so strong that he believed it to be the cause of the rift between his son and himself in December 1896, which led to Rudolf's departure for South America. All through that year, he said, he had avoided the assignment of his property by raising more money; but by April 1898, with Ingham coming almost daily to urge an assignment, his affairs had reached a state of crisis. One morning during the first week of April, he had told Ingham that "I could not see the sense of it as my liabilities were about $200,000 less than they were in 1896 and at best it would cost $100,000, to which he replied, let the creditors pay that. I said of course he knew well enough that I wouldn't have anything of that sort, and then he said, "You will make that very quick again, after the thing is over. The conversation, of course lasted longer, and I can't remember all; it is not material, I don't think, and he finally offered that he would manage it."

Ward: "That was the time when matters were very close and there was lots of hustling? During that time of storm and stress he approached you with that proposition?"

Dolge: "Yes sir, every day."

"To go into insolvency?"

"Yes sir."

"And that he would take charge and direction of it?"

"Yes sir."

"Did you finally tell him he might go ahead?"

"Yes sir. I said, if you think it best for all and the only thing that ought to be done, to go ahead."

Of Judge Hardin, Dolge testified that he had "met him on the street at Herkimer and said, 'Judge, I don't think I am doing the right thing now, I think it is all wrong,' and he said to me, 'O yes, you are; now don't lose courage at the last moment; you are in the hands of your friends and we will protect you and your son, and we have the bars all put up so that nobody can break in: you go home to Dolgeville and stay there and don't talk to anybody and have nothing to do with lawyers and let Mr. Ingham manage this thing."

The market value of the Dolge properties also figured in the testimony. Dolge placed it at a little over $3,000,000 and estimated his indebtedness to Judge Hardin, and National Herkimer County Bank, and the American Exchange Bank as $830,000. The wool he had shipped out had been applied to the debt, and reduced the amount a little.

Even then, Dolge's efforts to refinance the debt had continued. After being told by Ingham that he "was out of it and that the present owners had no use for me, I went to New York and saw my friends to get the money to pay those people, and get the property back and protect my other creditors, and I proposed a plan which was accepted by my friends and the attorney of most of the other creditors."

Ward: "That was Mr. Fletcher?"

Dolge: "Yes sir. According to which I was to raise about one million and have stock issued to the creditors to the amount of their claim, which was to be preferred shares, and I was to get the common stock and all of the profits made were to be applied on the purchase of the preferred stock before I was to get control, and, of course, when that was done the preferred stock was to go to me." When he went to Ingham, however, Dolge was told, "You are too late and can't have your property." Ingham had offered to set anywhere from $15,000 to $100,000 for Mrs. Dolge's benefit—to which Dolge had responded that there was no money that Ingham could give, since it belonged to the creditors.

Throughout the testimony, Dolge continued to express confidence that he could have weathered the storm. Here is Ward's question: "Did you, just about the 9th of April, 1898—did you have offers of funds which you refused, which would have been nearly sufficient to have carried you through the panic and your firm?"

Dolge: "Yes, sir."

Ward: "And you refused to take the funds for that purpose upon whose advice?"

Dolge: "Mr. Ingham's."

Ward: "Can you, if necessary, produce the parties from whom you had the offer of these funds?"

Dolge: "One man, a note broker, sat in my office all day Saturday waiting for me, knowing there was trouble, and told Mr. Wanckle that he could get us $70,000. I went to the telephone and talked with Mr. Ingham and he said 'No, don't talk with Mr. Chapman.' Mr. Chapman had told Mr. Wanckle that he could get us $70,000, and Mr. Clark of the American Exchange Bank was willing to help us if I could raise $70,000."

Ward: "How much would it have required to carry you through?"

Dolge: "It was a bad time and war was coming on, and it might be three or four months, and I would have had to have provided $140,000 for those months if we couldn't sell our property." Dolge added in answer to a further question, "If Mr. Ingham hadn't been in New York and talked to me as he had in those weeks, I am satisfied in my mind that nothing would have happened." Bitterly, he repeated what Ingham had told Rudolf—"Your father is a poor man now, that is all there is to it, and you must hustle for yourself the best you know how."

Ward: "I close the examination of Mr. Dolge."[7]

Fraud was never proved.

On May 6, 1899, Judge Hardin—with the air of a man whose patience has been sorely tried—made a statement of his own. "Dolge," he said, "is a visionary. He is an anarchist, an atheist, a Communist and an agnostic. When the proposition to put the Bible in the public schools of Dolgeville came up, he said that he didn't know whether the Bible was good for anything or not. His father wore the chain and ball for political offenses in Germany, and his own opinions are rabid. Yet this man does not hesitate to attack the characters of men like Mr. Ingham and myself, who have had the record of years of honest association with the people of this country and this State behind us."

Judge Hardin declared further that he would personally lose $10,000 as a result of giving Dolge Western Union stock to use as collateral. He would have agreed to Dolge's buying back his mills if Dolge had been able first to obtain the consent of the New York banks. Finally, he made a personal thrust: "A month ago (Dolge) went around saying he would put an end to his troubles after the German method—commit suicide. He was drinking hard. He would put his hand down on the table hard. 'I will commit suicide,' he said. 'That's the way a German ends his troubles, and *I WILL NOT GO ALONE*!" Hardin concluded by saying that Dolge had built a $75,000 house when he owed money all over the country, and that it would never bring more than $5,000; that he had also spent $47,000 on a clubhouse, $60,000 on useless grading of streets, and had sunk $44,000 as a fad in his paper, the *Dolgeville Herald*—when he knew he was operating on borrowed capital, "which he could not hope to pay back."[8]

Alfred Dolge had believed he could pay it back.

His error, as he saw it later, was in not having acted "as the cool clear-headed straightforward business man, as which I had been known to the community for thirty years. I had lost my head and trusted two, as I believed, stronger men and honest, sincere friends."[9]

According to an 1898 clipping, "Edward Burns of the American Exchange National Bank of New York purchased recently all the real and personal property contained in the felt plant in the interest of a syndicate comprising some of the large creditors of Alfred Dolge and Son. A company now in the process of organization that will not only operate the felt mills, but also the mills of the Daniel Green Felt Shoe Company, and the two principal industries of the village will be placed under one management and one business head. It was generally supposed that Alfred Dolge would be the business head of the corporation, but this place is already filled by Schuyler R. Ingham of Little Falls."[10]

Two small items summed up the matter. "The felt factory started Tuesday morning with a force of about 50 hands. The hours of labor are 10 instead of 9½ as formerly."

On the same page of the paper is this item: "A short while ago Collector Wood levied on a piano, a table, and some other household furniture belonging to Mrs. Alfred Dolge in lieu of unpaid taxes. The furniture was valued at about $700, while the amount of the unpaid tax was $92.50. Not a dozen people were present! The articles were finally struck down to E. A. Brown for $125. He represented "Clara", a servant in the Dolge family for years.[11]

The mopping up had begun almost before the milk was spilt. Lawyers crowded the village, attending to the details.

Hugo Dolge, on hearing the news by way of a telegram from Dolgeville, immediately made an assignment of the woolen company in Dryden. His liabilities were said to have been $15,000, against $12,000 in assets.[12]

Not quite a year later, on March 24, 1899, large blocks of unencumbered real estate were sold under the direction of William N. Kernan, the assignee. Property which Alfred Dolge had valued at just under $200,000 went for $9,000. The Platt property on Main Street, whose asking price had been $6,000, went to M. G. Bronner of Little Falls on a bid of $930. Village lots whose asking value had been $300 to $500 went for three and five dollars. The Z. G. Brockett farm, purchased by Dolge for $10,000, was sold to Julius Breckwoldt for $1,210. The Reuben Faville farm, including High Falls Park, in which Dolge had invested $16,000, went to M. G. Bronner, acting on behalf of the felt trust, for $1,225. The trust likewise acquired the rights to the water power next to the felt factories, for a total of $1,200. The factory lands had been mortgaged for $300,000 to Judge Hardin as trustee.

The stone quarry at Inghams Mills was sold for $165.

Calvin Brockett acquired a block of swampland behind his residence for a bid of $33.[13]

At the autoharp factory, thousands of instruments complete except for stringing were burned. The rest of the industries continued to operate, in one form or another. But the initial thrust and impetus were gone. As for the innovations—the pension and profit-sharing plans—yet another clipping sums up the matter: "Profit sharing has no standing with the new owners of the works."[14]

So that was the end of the first venture in social security, and good riddance so far as the new owners were concerned.

CHAPTER 8
AFTERMATH

April in the foothills of the Adirondacks—patches of dirty snow, rushing water, tracings of ice, delicate tones of brown, taupe, green, and gray in the sunlight. The lakes have talked and groaned their way free of ice. Spring comes late here, but already that thin sunlight seems to call for rejoicing.

That was what made it hard to bear.

There was an extreme feeling against bankruptcy. Just two years later, the papers would carry an account of the suicide of a Charles Potter, who was so despondent over going bankrupt that he killed himself with a rifle. The feeling both for and against Dolge ran high. His failure was blamed for the death of Philip Helmer, whose large farm Dolge had bought, graded, and laid out into streets and lots: "The blow," according to one newspaper account, "undoubtedly hastened his death, as it did also that of Mrs. Helmer."[1] Young men who had looked forward confidently to a college education under Dolge's encouragement were left without even a job. Fancher Youker, who later became a fine newspaper man, was one of these.

In newspapers throughout the region, the affair was being discussed at length. According to the *Utica Sunday Tribune*, "Alfred Dolge is very much depressed and broken down over the failure and has remained continuously at his residence on Dolge Avenue since his return to Dolgeville Monday. The one object of his life seems to be the building up of the village that bears his honored name, and to have all his hopes shattered and blasted when at the very moment success seemed to crown his life-work has been a strain that Alfred Dolge, strong as he is mentally and physically, is compelled to give in to. His esteemed wife whose many kind and charitable acts have won for her the love, respect and esteem of every man, woman and child in the village, is prostrated by the shock and is now under medical attendance."

The *Buffalo Express* described Alfred Dolge as "much the best known and most interesting man in American industrial life. . . . He came to this country a poor man, and he has succeeded not only in building up a number of important enterprises, but is carrying into practice ideas which have been designed to do justice between employer and workman."

The *Utica Sunday Journal* declared, "His system of profit sharing with his employees was unique in this country." And according to the *Carbondale Leader*, in Pennsylvania, "A review of the facts in regard to the Dolge failure shows that it was not because of the profit sharing system the firm went under. The reason was that Mr. Dolge had too many irons in the fire."

And what of the people who had been defrauded of their promised pensions, who were never to receive the old age benefits Dolge had so long striven for, who had lost their share in the control of the factories he had built? One man remembered that for years afterward, he would rush out and spit at "Old Schuyler" (Ingham) whenever he drove down the street in his carriage. And in that bleak April of the year 1899, eight hundred of Alfred Dolge's former employees organized a farewell to the man they had been told had sold them down the river.

The Turnhall he had built, the vast magnificent Turnhall which had helped to bankrupt him, was decorated with branches of evergreens, giving off the woodland perfume that Germans love. Lights suspended from the high ceiling illuminated the place as the crowd waited. The silence, people who were there remembered afterward, was like the stillness of a great funeral. They recalled earlier meetings, when Dolge had spoken of raising wages, reducing their hours, or of how the earning-sharing plan was to work. There had been cheers then. Would they cheer tonight?

On the stage, the curtains opened. Six men in the uniforms of the hose company Dolge had founded marched on the stage, their faces stern. And from the silent hall there went up a roar of applause, as though a hurricane wind had struck. Men and women clapped until their hands stung, and shouted until their throats ached, as Alfred Dolge appeared before them for the last time.

The oldest of the firemen, Willard Roberts, was speaking: ". . . true and loyal friend, farewell."

As the applause died away a second time, Alfred Dolge began to speak. "I do not object of having my efforts in Dolgeville called a dream. My dream was to build up a village, yea, a city which should stand out as a worthy product of American civilization and progress, industrially, socially, intellectually, artistically, and in a humanitarian sense. . . . The unkempt and unwashed . . . disappeared from our streets, vulgar language was used less and less by those who worked in our factories." He went on quietly, enumerating the steps by which he had made his dreams a reality—the clubhouse in place of the saloon, the festivals and pastimes that had enlivened a sleepy little town, the kindergarten that educated the parents as much as it did the child; the Academy with its cooking, sewing, manual training, and music; the public library. He spoke of future possibilities—electric cars to the valley and to the beautiful Auskerada lakes; an eight-hour day; a university, theatre, opera, public gardens, an earthly paradise in the midst of these northern forests. He spoke of how his own labor pension and insurance system had been recognized by the government of Germany "when introducing compulsory labor pension laws which are now in force there."

Then he went on to more painful matters. "I trusted my 'friends' implicitly. They have done their work well. With a cunning which would be a credit to Lucifer himself, they fastened the stigma on my oldest son, that, at least before the world, he appeared to be the person who had ruined me, who had turned against his own father, mother and brothers—while as a matter of fact, George A. Hardin and Schuyler R. Ingham had induced the young man to sign a document which empowered Ingham to strike the fatal blow at me whenever he saw fit to. Of course Ingham had told the inexperienced young man that he would use this power only for the benefit of the creditors, myself, and Dolgeville, or else Rudolf would have never signed the document.

"Today," Dolge went on, "Ingham is the chairman of the Executive Committee of the Felt Trust which owns my factories and business. They attacked my wife. The tax collector sold every piece of her furniture. Ingham offered Mrs. Dolge a bribe of fifty or sixty thousand dollars, which he finally raised to $100,000 to me, if I would keep quiet. In both cases our answer was that no amount of money could tempt us to the atrocious crime which had been committed against me, my creditors, and the people of Dolgeville. They caught me in a moment of weakness caused by exhaustion and overwork, they did not lose the opportunity but took me by the throat, tied me hand and foot, threw me in the gutter and invited their helpers and underlings to spit in my face."

Would Dolge ever again rise above such bitterness, which can eat away at a soul? His concluding words were calmer: "Although my books have been examined over and over again, showed a suplus of $1,300,000 over all liabilities, I leave Dolgeville a poor man, saddled with an enormous indebtedness; but I go away, head erect, knowing that not all my labor has been lost. I leave my footprints here which cannot be erased whatever may come.

"Goodbye! Goodbye!"[2]

After he had finished speaking, no one moved for what seemed an endless time. Then slowly, as in a pageant, the members of the hose company came down from the stage. Dolge began shaking hands with friends and neighbors; a few were there whom he refused to greet. Gradually the crowd moved downstairs to the dining room. The fire chief, Paul Franz, was toastmaster, injecting as much humor as he could into a funereal occasion. Dolge declared that he intended to go west—to where, sitting perhaps in some log cabin out in Montana, he would think of them all.[3]

Was Dolge an honest man? Most thought so. Some were not sure. Some felt he didn't owe a cent to the town, that when all was sold as planned for a tenth of its worth, business would start up again and all would be happy. Almost all.

They said he never came back.

Some went to join him in the West. Adolf Horn, Martin Gardner, Franz Diederich, Chauncey Mosher, Gustav Freygang, Ben Parker, Paul Diedrich, Charles Millet, Michael Holian, and Andrew Volts were among them. Later, Gustav Freygang and his wife Rosa returned east, as did others.

In May 1899, the great sad house on Dolge Avenue stood denuded of furniture, its fine parquet floors gleaming without rugs. Friends came to pay their respects in a bare house. It was the sweetest time of the year in that countryside; outside, the waters of Tegahuhharoghwe dashed foaming white toward the Mohawk, as Alfred Dolge and his family took leave of the town that had been named for him. In California, beginning with two carloads of wine that he had brought with him from New York, he launched a wholesale wine business. With the friends who joined him from Dolgeville, he soon had a new felt factory in operation at a place that for a time was also known as Dolgeville—though eventually it was engulfed by the nearby town of Alhambra, of which it then became a part. He specialized in covering piano hammers. The felt was dried by solar heat in 1905. Later Dolge sold pianos, acquired an interest in an orange grove near Covina—and made money.

He never quite lost touch with the place he had left behind. In 1904, the Canada Lakes venture he had envisioned came into being. The *Fulton County Republican* for October 6 of that year carried the headline: "Canada Lake Property Falls Into *Good Hands*: Purchased by Caroga Lumber and Land Company of This City—Beauty of Resort Not to Be Marred." Exactly as Dolge had planned, the company proposed to sell cottage lots and lumber off the south side. They also foresaw the possibility of a trolley between Dolgeville and Gloversville. At the same auction, land in Salisbury and Stratford which, when Dolge acquired it, had been one of the largest tracts ever sold in the state—about four square miles in all—was sold to the representative of a consortium of lumber dealers.[4]

In 1907 the Giese Wire Company closed, with the death of Herman Giese. The felt industry was moved to Glenville, Connecticut and Franklin, Massachusetts.

The Dolgeville Felt Shoe Company, which had begun manufacturing in the old Turnhall in 1902 under William Menge and Frank Engel, had many years of prosperity ahead of it. The Daniel Green Company became known across the nation, and would go on thriving in the years to come.[5]

A letter to George Smith, editor of the *Dolgeville Republican*, on August 3, 1915, showed the man Alfred Dolge had become since what he referred to as the "catastrophe . . . of April, 1898." After thanking the editor for a paper that "aroused pleasant memories of bygone days, the days of my young manhood, when I was full of dreams and ideals, willing and ready to bring most any sacrifice to make those dreams a reality," he said, "Although I live here in paradise, I cannot help feeling as if I were in exile." He told of the new Dolgeville, and its annexation to Alhambra. "I did not regret that," he confessed, "because my heart was ever with old Dolgeville on the foothills of the Adirondacks so strongly that I never could warm up to any particular interest in the new Dolgeville on the foothills of the Sierra Madre. Sitting on my veranda in twilight hours, I often dream of how useful I might have been in old Dolgeville during the past sixteen years, had I been permitted to carry out my plans, and good Mrs. Dolge will talk about the thousands of trees which she planted with her own hands on that hillside back of our old home, and which is now named after the man who destroyed my work to enrich himself."

That hillside once Summer House Hill was now Schuyler Ingham Park. In 1921, briefly, Alfred Dolge and his wife Anna were once again in the Adirondacks. Though they could not bring themselves to return to Dolgeville, they did visit Little Falls, and some of the "boys" from Hose Company No. 1 went to see their old friend and patron. "I am a sentimentalist," he told them. "I could not go to Dolgeville, much as I would like to see my dear friends there. It would break my heart. I did not care for money, except for the good uses I might make with it. To make a lot of money is not the main thing in life. So far my good wife has devoted her life to me. Now, in the few years that remain, I am going to devote my life to her. We are now on a last long trip around the world. We are going to be very happy and have a good time."[6]

And so they did, in the six months that remained to them.

Alfred Dolge died in Milan on January 5, 1922, at the age of seventy-three. His wife was to outlive him by many years. In a Christian Science home in the vicinity of Hollywood, she surrounded herself with pictures of her children and grandchildren "unto the third generation," and her memories. A friend who visited her in 1934 was amazed at her memory of Dolgeville people.[7] She died in 1941 at the home of her son Fritz's widow (who changed his name to Grant Emerson Dolge), and her ashes are beside her husband's in the Dolgeville cemetery, where she erected a monument to his memory.[8]

Of their sons, Fritz or Grant Emerson, who survived his father, died young in Oxford, Massachusetts. Henry settled in Los Angeles, and William in San Francisco as an accountant and financier. Ernst was trained as a horticulturist and ran a fruit ranch in Los Angeles County; later he cultivated Douglas fir in Tacoma, Washington. Rudolf's career in South America was a distinguished one. A moving spirit in the Orinoco Company, a founder of the Sociedad de Sciencias Naturales, first president of the Venezuelan section of the Pan American Society, and a managing representative of the Standard Oil Company, he cultivated an interest in the literature and history of Venezuela and remained an unflagging champion of good relations between South America and the United States.[9]

On January 29, 1922, the "boys" of the Alfred Dolge Hose Company held a memorial service arranged by Wyman Dooley, Fire Chief. The principal address on that day was given by John C. Freund, who had been editor of the *Dolgeville Herald*, and who had returned from New York City for the occasion. What he said makes a fitting epitaph:

"The sun is shining brightly in this beautiful industrial town, snow covered. You breathe the keen, bracing air of the Adirondacks. People are out on skis and snowshoes. . . .

"Alfred Dolge was largely responsible for the prominent position which Dolgeville took not alone in the industries of the country, but because it was a point from which emanated propaganda for industrial insurance, pension for labor, profit-sharing and other methods of dealing justly with workers. Then regarded as Utopian, these methods are coming more and more to be adopted—indeed, some of them have become law in certain States.

"It is not an easy thing for a man who was associated as I was with Alfred Dolge to come here after nearly thirty years, to see the wonderful development of what was once a half dead little country village of a few hundred people, twelve miles from a railroad, developed into a thriving industrial city of nearly four thousand inhabitants, and know that the man who devised it all, who built it up, passed on thousands of miles away in a strange land, no longer connected with it, having lost his all.

"If Alfred Dolge did not realize what he had hoped for himself, for his family; if he did not leave any large fortune, which is often more of a curse than a blessing; if to the very last his life was one of struggle, of care, he won out in the larger sense, in the sense of duty done, in the sense that there is no finer, no nobler work on this earth than to undertake something which will give honest employment, bread and a home to hundreds, for the home is the basis of civilization."[10]

When my husband was in his first year at Colgate University, he mentioned Alfred Dolge to a professor of German. The professor answered, "Alfred Dolge—oh yes, I know him. He was a great man."

NOTE ON SOURCES

For nearly thirty years I have been Historian of Dolgeville and the Town of Manheim. It was my father-in-law, Paul Franz, who first interested me in the career of Alfred Dolge. Rita Rockwell, librarian of the Dolgeville Public Library, gave me access to many Dolge papers, and I opened and catalogued the contents of the cornerstone of the Union Free School. In addition, Supervising Principal Emory Tooly of the Dolgeville Central School, gave me a number of old papers and letters concerned with the school. Claire Vogel gave me a history of the Dolge family preserved by Henry Dolge, to whom she was related by marriage. Herbert Guenther of Schenectady, nephew of Alfred Dolge, most generously sent me pictures, letters, and an account of the early days as he remembered them. For three years I taught an Adult Education course in Folklore and Local History. Many of those participating had lived during the time of Alfred Dolge, and their contributions are acknowledged in the references that follow. In addition, I have drawn on a manuscript autobiography of Dolge, submitted to *McClure's Magazine* on March 20, 1906, and on his three published books: *Economic Theories as Practically Applied in the Factories of Alfred Dolge and Son at Dolgeville, N. Y.* (Dolgeville: Herald Publishing Company, 1896), *History of a Crime* (Los Angeles, 1900), and *Pianos and Their Makers* (Covina, California: Covina Publishing Company, 1911). Much information is provided by the *Dolgeville Herald*, the *Dolgeville Republican*, and the *Scrutinizer*, an annual publication, all of which appeared in Dolge's time, and by the annual addresses of Dolge to his employees as reprinted by the Associated Press and the United Press in 1895 and 1896.

FOOTNOTES

CHAPTER 1

1. Recollections of Daniel Sullivan.

2. Recollections of Elizabeth Heller, Proctor Spofford, and William Faville, including a map of Brockett's Bridge in 1871 drawn by the latter with Lou Snell.

3. Recollections of Lafayette Hewitt.

4. "Alfred Dolge's Farewell," *Dolgeville Herald*, May 4, 1899, p. 4.

5. K. F. Reinhardt, *Germany, 2,000 Years* (New York: Frederick Ungar, 1961), Vol. II, p. 518.

6. An account of Christian Dolge's part in the Revolution was handed down by members of the family:

"Armed with nothing but clubs, flails, and scythes, the young revolutionaries had seemed close to victory in Dresden, the capital of Saxony, but were then quickly put down by Prussian troops under Prince Wilhelm. Their leader, the twenty-eight-year-old Christian Dolge, was imprisoned at Pleissenburg Fortress at Leipzig and sentenced to death. His devoted wife Augusta was allowed to visit him, however, and brought him a hacksaw blade concealed in a fat liver sausage. With it he sawed through three iron bars to the rhythm of the military band as it played reveille, using the butter from the thickly spread sandwiches Augusta had brought to grease the saw. He tied himself to a rope made of bedclothes and escaped, but fell and broke an arm, a leg, and his nose when the makeshift rope broke before he could descend from the second story window. He managed painfully to swim across the moat and to clamber up the bank, where he fainted and was recaptured. Thus he was prevented from joining Carl Schurz and Gottfried Kinkel, two other leaders who had planned to escape from Prussia to England. He spent five years in Waldheim prison, shackled much of the time and suffering great hardship. Meanwhile, his sentence had been reduced to life imprisonment."

Efforts to obtain a pardon for Christian Dolge are said to have included this picturesque bit of pleading: "At the wedding of the then crown prince of Saxony, later known as King Albert of Saxony, to a princess of Sweden, the members of a prominent old aristocratic family, whose only son, like Grandfather had been in the army, and had participated actively in the Revolution, arranged to have a dove descend on the lap of the newly wed crown princess as their carriage was slowly driving through the streets of Dresden, with a petition tied around the dove's neck, pleading for the life of the prisoners who had been condemned to death."

7. Alfred Dolge, "Autobiography" (manuscript).

8. Reinhardt, *op. cit.*, p. 518.

9. Alfred's brothers left Germany eventually; Hugo to Dolgeville, Carl Bruno going to

New York and Henry Arthur to Venezuela. His father was not permitted to leave for a time. Bruno eventually became head of the engraving department of *Harper's*.

10. Dolge, "Autobiography."

11. *Ibid.*

12. *Ibid.*

13. *Ibid.*

14. *Ibid.* Also, cornerstone, Union Free School, 1887.

15. Dolge, "Autobiography," p. 13.

16. *Dolgeville Herald*, August 29, 1895 p. 1.

17. Dolge, "Autobiography."

18. George A. Hardin, *History of Herkimer County* (Syracuse: D. Mason and Co., 1893), pp. 334-335. The tannery was built by Major D. B. Winton in 1830 and became known as the Herkimer County Tannery. It burned in December 1845, was rebuilt the next year with the same walls. Isaac Corse of New York—later Corse, Lapham, Thorn and Co. and still later Watson and Thorn—operated it. From 1856 to 1861 Oliver Ladue was manager. The tannery ceased work in 1872.

CHAPTER 2

1. "Dolgeville's History" *Scrutinizer*, January 27, 1894, p. 3.

2. *Ibid.*

3. *Ibid.*

4. Dolge, "Autobiography."

5. *Journal and Courier, Industrial ed.* (Little Falls), December 1895, pp. 31-32

6. Herbert Guenther, nephew of Alfred Dolge, gave some vivid details of the changeover to electric lighting in his reminiscences written in 1957: "The original lighting in the stable was oil lamps with round silvered mirror reflectors, bracket mounted. When Mr. Dolge installed the Edison dynamo in the factory areas, the stable was one of the first buildings, other than the factory, to be converted to electric illumination. "Old Bill Platt" was foreman. . . . Bill was so perturbed with the brilliancy of this new lighting setup that he said, 'Alfred, you sure as hell are going to burn up the barn with so much light.' Another said, 'The lights won't never be worth a damn; you can't blow 'em out.' "

7. Alfred Dolge, *Pianos and Their Makers* (Covina, California: Covina Publishing Company, 1911) p. 101.

8. Nelson Greene, ed., *History of the Mohawk Valley* (Chicago: S. J. Clarke, 1925) Vol. IV, p. 772; also George A. Hardin, *History of Herkimer County*, *op. cit.* p. 339. Material on Julius Breckwoldt was also furnished by his granddaughter, Mrs. Edwin Vosburgh.

9. Recollections of Catherine Green. The famous old trademark of a lamb and a felt slipper appeared on what were called Alfred Dolge Felt Shoes; later the name was changed to Daniel Green Felt Shoes, and still later the Daniel Green Comfy trademark dropped the lamb motif. Daniel Green himself died in 1891.

10. *Dolgeville Herald*, May, 1889, p. 1.

11. Recollections of Ernest Stone.

12. Hardin, *op. cit.*, p. 336; also recollections of Mrs. George Jones who circulated a

petition; also *Scrutinizer*, January 27, 1894, *op. cit.*

13. Alfred Dolge, *Economic Theories as Practically Applied in the Factories of Alfred Dolge and Son at Dolgeville, N. Y.* (Dolgeville: Herald Publishing Company, 1896) p. 56.

14. Silas R. Kimm, "Tales of Brockett's Bridge and Salisbury 70 Years Ago," *Evening Times* (Little Falls), March 25, 1944.

15. *Journal and Courier, Industrial ed.* (Little Falls), December 1895, p. 25.

16. Dolge, *Economic Theories, op. cit.* p. 27.

17. *Dolgeville Herald*, June 10, 1897.

18. Recollections of Alva Gardner, daughter of Dr. Spofford.

19. Recollections of William Menge, III.

20. Recollections of Ernest Stone.

21. Recounted by Lorenz Franz, son of Paul Franz.

CHAPTER 3

1. Dolge, "Autobiography."

2. *Dolgeville Republican*, September 23, 1948, p. 3.

3. Dolge, "Earnings vs. Profit Sharing," *Social Economist*, January 1892, reprinted in *Economic Theories, Op. cit.*, p. 175.

4. "Earnings Division System," in *Economic Theories, op. cit.* pp. 233-240.

5. "The 8 Hour System," 1886, in *Economic Theories, op. cit.*, p. 64.

6. "Protection of Home Industries," 1888, in *Economic Theories, op. cit.*, p. 79.

7. "Workingmen and the Tariff," 1888, in *Economic Theories, op. cit.*, p. 97.

8. "Protection of Home Industries," *op. cit.* p. 82.

9. "Development of Mind and Muscle" (address to Dolgeville *Turnverein*, August 29, 1885), in *Economic Theories*, p. 140.

10. "The Culture Mission", in *Economic Theories*, p. 211.

11. *Dolgeville Herald*, August 1, 1895, p. 8.

12. *Journal and Courier, Industrial ed., op. cit.*, p. 28.

13. I. M. Rubinow, *Quest for Security* (New York: Holt, 1934), p. 596.

14. Dolge, "Earnings vs. Profit Sharing", *Social Economist*, January 1892 reprinted in *Economic Theories. op. cit.* p. 169.

15. *Scrutinizer*, January 22, 1887, p. 4.

16. Dolge, "Autobiography."

17. "Development of Mind and Muscle," in *Economic Theories, op. cit.*, p. 137.

18. *Dolgeville Herald*, July 20, 1894.

19. It was the custom to turn out commemorative steins for some of these occasions. Made of a bluish gray native clay decorated with a design in delft blue, they were usually straight sided, but one (undated) has the shape of a small fat cask. They were made by the C.N.Y. Pottery in Utica for the 1894 *Turnfest*. The *Utica Daily Press* for July 26, 1894,

observes: "These mugs are somewhat larger than they were six years ago—they have grown, no doubt. They are of stoneware . . . and bear this inscription: '25 bezirk's turnfest, West New York, Dolgeville, N.Y. 1894: F.F.S.T. & 11. The letters stand for 'fresh, free, strong and true,' and '11' has reference to the 11th commandment, one that is never broken by turners."

Many of the German families treasured two or three fine old steins, which might be displayed on a dining room sideboard. The finest was a gallon-size engraved "Presented by the B.T.V. to the D.T.V., 1888," and was used by the Dolgeville *Turnverein* for some time, passed hand to hand and, we assume, mouth to mouth. It is dark blue decorated with a seated dwarf, possibly representing Perkeo of Heidelberg fame.

Once in a while a special jug or bottle would be commissioned. The William Jennings Saloon of Dolgeville had a little gray jug trimmed in dull blue and ornamented with a fat gentleman bending half over and being kicked by a kicking machine, a wheel with boots attached. Conical match holders of this same stoneware are in existence; they held long matches, to be scraped on their rought sides.

20. Recollections of Rosa Franz Freygang.

21. The banquet menus printed for the prosperous years had caricatures of the Dolges, the employees, Grossvater Dolge's bears, and the factories. Their contents bear witness to the lavishness with which the Germans liked to entertain. It was the fashion of the age. It was also very German. The dinner menu for 1889 read as follows:

Nudelsuppe

Celery Fish Olives

Kartoffeln Salat

Roast

Entenbraten

Allerei Schmorkartoffeln

Compot Kaffee

Weifsweine

Feltinger Craacher

Rudesheimer

Rothwane

St. Julien Chambertin Californier

Liqueur

For January 29, 1893, the menu appears somewhat Americanized:

Chicken Soup

Olives Celery

Salmon Trout w. Potatoes

Tenderloin, Mushrooms and Fried Potatoes

Roast Lamb with Potatoes Croquettes

Dessert Salad

Rice Pudding

Nuts Fruits

Bread, Butter

Cheese Coffee

California Zinfandell

Mosel

Winninger

Geisenheimer

Ungar

Oedenburrger Natur wein

Linck's Blume
Diverse Liquors

Champagne Benedictine

Chartreuse
Cognac

The wine list was never slighted!

22. Dolge, "Autobiography."

23. *Dolgeville Herald*, November 21, 1895, p. 1.

24. The German games were described in my folklore class.

25. Recollections of Edwin Hopson.

26. Dolge, "Autobiography."

CHAPTER 4

1. Herbert Guenther, "Reminiscences of Fulton County" (unpublished manuscript, 1957).

2. Recollections of Emogene Bliss, over 100 years old when interviewed.

3. Guenther, "Reminiscences."

4. "High Falls Park," n.d. (brochure of the Little Falls and Dolgeville Railroad)

5. *Evening Times* (Little Falls), July 1, 1924.

6. Recollections of Mrs. Warren Reardon, Sr.

7. Recollections of Freda Cunningham.

8. Austin Chase of Little Falls: *Utica Press*, January 19, 1966.

9. Recollections of Freda Cunningham.

10. *Dolgeville Herald*, July 18, 1895, p. 8.

11. *Ibid.* January 9, 1896.

12. *Dolgeville Herald*, November 7, 1895, p. 8, and register of Guenther Hotel.

13. *Dolgeville Herald*, January 9, 1896, p. 8.

14. Recollections of Le Roy Loomis.

15. The property was described as follows: Great Lot 59 on the south side of Canada Lake, Great Lot 60 on the north side, Great Lot 65 including West Lake, Great Lot 66 on the south side, including the Canada Lake outlet and Lily Lake (from Simmons and Van Newst), Subdivisions 5 and 7 in the Great Lot 57 (from Claffin) including all of Green Lake. *Fulton County Republican* (Johnstown), October 6, 1904, p. 8.

16. *Scrutinizer*, January 26, 1895.

17. "Forestry," in *Economic Theories, op. cit.*, p. 46.

18. *Ibid.*, p. 47.

19. "Aughstagradi, A Tale of the Auskeradas" (New York: Auskerada Park Club, 1897). Loaned by Charles Dolge.

20. Recollections of Bea Halliday, Canada Lake, N. Y.

21. Recollections of Emogene Bliss.
22. Recollections of Lorenz Franz.
23. Recollections of Emogene Bliss.
24. Three typical German kuchen recipes follow with their sources:

STOELLEN *Mrs. Joseph Buckley*
1½ cakes of yeast
1 pint of milk scalded and cooled
2½ cups of flour
1 T. sugar

Put the yeast and the sugar in the milk when it is luke warm. Beat the flour in and let rise 1 hour. Now take ½ cup of butter, 1 cup of sugar and cream together. Add 3 eggs and beat well into this batter. Put all together and add 1 tsp. salt, the grated rind of a lemon, 2 cups of raisins, currants, ½ cup of nuts sliced, a few drained and sliced maraschino cherries. Flour the fruit. Now add flour to stir stiff, knead a little while, make it into 2 loaves and let rise until double in bulk on a greased cookie sheet. Bake at 350° and dust with confectionery sugar.

CURRANT TEA RING *Mrs. Conrad Hurth*
1½ cup milk scalded
1 cup sugar
½ cup butter
1½ yeast cakes
3 eggs
1 tsp. salt
Grated rind of two lemons
5½ cups of flour
½ cup of flour to knead

Scald the milk; add the yeast when it is luke warm. Add sugar and butter to milk and yeast. Beat eggs and add some of the flour to the batter and then the eggs. Add rest of flour and salt. Let rise and punch down. Cut the dough into two pieces and roll ¼ inch thick. Spread with cut up dried fruits or some marmalade, brown sugar or white, and dots of butter, and then roll. Pinch the ends together and curve the crescents. Nestle them within their own embrace on a cookie sheet, cover, and let rise again. Bakc 50 minutes at 350°.

Apfelkuchen may be made with a cookie dough or a bread dough base. (I prefer the latter.)

APFELKUCHEN *Mrs. Conrad Hurth, Mrs. Gustav Freygang, and Mrs. Paul Franz*
1½ yeast cakes
1 cup milk scalded
1 T. sugar
¼ cup butter
2 eggs
½ tsp. salt
3½ cups sifted flour

Make a dough, knead a few minutes, and let rise 2 hours. Roll it out to ¼-inch thick. This is enough for 3 pans, 9″ × 13″. Brush with butter. Sprinkle with sugar, cut apples in eighths, and press in dough sharp edge down. Put more butter, sugar, and cinnamon on top. Plums may be used instead, omitting the cinnamon. Streiselkuchen is made with the same dough only sprinkled with a mixture of ⅓ cup flour, 2 T. brown sugar, and cinnamon, and dotted with butter. When baking with fruit on top, let rise and bake for 20 minutes uncovered and then 10 minutes covered with another pan to cook the fruit.

CHAPTER 5

1. Recollections of Anna Schroeder.

2. *First Union Free School of Dolgeville, N.Y.* (New York: William Knowles, 1888) p. 4.

3. *Ibid.*

4. *Ibid.* p. 5. The founders of the School Society were H. E. Brayton, Carl Dedicke, Edward Dedicke, John Dern, Alfred Dolge, August Dolge, Henry A. Dolge, Hugo Dolge, Carl Fallier, Paul Fallier, J. Goerke, G. Guenther, August Haas, H. Hardt, F. Harnischfelger, G. Horn, F. Illing, Joseph Koch, Albert Kramer, H. Mueller, John Penn, N. Rosen, A. Wegner, F. Wolff.

5. *Ibid.*, p. 6.

6. *Ibid*, p. 12. Members of the building committee were Alfred Dolge, Peter J. Dunckel, Frank Faville, Henry Faville, Howard Spencer, Dr. A. G. Barney, Theodore Sanford, Wheeler Knapp.

7. *Ibid.*, p. 12.

8. *Ibid.*, p. 34. The cornerstone's contents included a handwritten history of Dolgeville by J. B. Koetteritz; products of the felt mills; piano hammers; a census of the town for 1887; typed minutes of the proceedings of the School Society (of interest since one of the earliest typewriters must have been acquired by Dolge); many photographs and newspapers.

9. *Scrutinizer*, January 22, 1887. This little paper, half humorous, printed Dolge's annual address and presented many of his viewpoints. This first issue strongly supported education.

10. *First Union Free School of Dolgeville, N.Y., op. cit.*

11. Old records left in the Dolgeville Central School, and donated by Supervising Principal Emory Tooly.

12. Silas C. Kimm, "School Society Formed," *Evening Times* (Little Falls), April 8, 1944.

13. *Souvenir of the Dedication of the New Academy* (Dolgeville, N. Y.: Dolgeville School Society, August 30, 1890), p. 15. Donated by Gertrude Thomas.

14. Dolge, *Economic Theories*, *op. cit.*, pp. 159-160.

15. Kindergarten booklets donated by Beatrice Wagner, who made them at age 5 under Miss Rust's directions. Her brother, Aaron Wagner of Mohawk, is the source of the statement that Dolgeville had the first public kindergarten in New York State.

16. *Souvenir of Dedication*, *op. cit.*, pp. 39-48.

17. *Ibid.*, pp. 15-16.

18. Edwin Hopson, "History of Education in Dolgeville", *Evening Times* (Little Falls) December 1, 1954, p. 3.

19. Letter to Board of Education, August 13, 1895, sent by School Society after public rejection of $850 for support of a kindergarten.

20. Edwin Hopson, *op. cit.*

21. *Souvenir of Dedication*, *op. cit.*, pp. 8, 9.

22. *Ibid.*, p. 27

23. *Ibid.*, pp. 39-48.

CHAPTER 6

1. *History of a Crime.* (Los Angeles, 1900), p. 5. Though unsigned, this book is clearly the work of Alfred Dolge. Many copies were destroyed. Two remain in Dolgeville.

2. Dolge. *Economic Theories, op. cit.*, p. 23.

3. Recollections of Ernest Stone; also, Nelson Greene, *History of the Mohawk Valley, op. cit.* Vol. IV, pp. 818-821.

4. *History of a Crime, op. cit.*, pp. 5, 6.

5. *Scrutinizer*, January 31, 1891, p. 3.

6. Recollections of Proctor Spofford.

7. *Journal and Courier, Industrial ed.* , (Little Falls) *op. cit.* p. 26.

8. Rudolf was educated at Hoboken Academy, the Leipzig Gymnasium and Cooper Union. Also, "Our Rudolf Married", *Dolgeville Herald*, March 16, 1893, p. 1.

9. *Scrutinizer*, January 26, 1895, p. 2.

10. *Dolgeville Republican*, April 23, 1898, p. 1.

11. Dolge, *Economic Theories, op cit.*, p. 206.

12. *Journal and Courier, Industrial Edition* (Little Falls) *op. cit.*, p. 27.

CHAPTER 7

1. *Dolgeville Republican*, March 27, 1947, reprint from Caracas, Venezuela *Journal.*

2. "Souvenir Supplement," *Dolgeville Herald*, February 10, 1898, p. 1.

3. *Ibid.*, p. 8.

4. Recollections of Anna Schroeder.

5. *Dolgeville Herald*, May 4, 1899, p. 4.

6. *History of a Crime, op. cit.*, p. 6.

7. *Dolgeville Herald*, April 27, 1899.

8. *Dolgeville Republican*, May 6, 1899, p. 1. (In rebuttal, the following appears *History of a Crime*; "George A. Hardin died April 13, 1901. During the last 28 years of his life he had no other visible source of income than his salary of $10,000 a year. Hardin was never connected with any business enterprise, except as stockholder in the National Herkimer County Bank and the active part he took in wrecking the firm of Alfred Dolge & Son. He left an estate valued at about $800,000."

9. *History of a Crime*, p. 24.

10. Newspaper clipping headed "Dolgeville" and dated September 10, 1898; from a scrapbook loaned by George Lyon.

11. *Dolgeville Republican*, September 10, 1898, p. 1.

12. *Dolgeville Republican*, April 23, 1898, p. 1.

13. "Great Slump in Values—Dolgeville Real Estate Sold for a Song," *Saturday Globe* (Utica), March 23, 1899.

14. Clipping dated September 10, 1899. It reads further, "75 policies of insurance at time of failure, 4 men on pension of half pay at time of failure, many had several hundred dollars on endowment books."

CHAPTER 8

1. Accounts from scrapbook loaned by George Lyon.

2. *Dolgeville Herald*, May 4, 1899, p. 4.

3. *Ibid.*

4. The company, which purchased it through attorney Dewitt C. Moore for $29,600, consisted of David A. Wells, James S. Ireland, Postmaster Cyrus Durey of Johnstown, and Supervisor Frank Sherman of Caroga. In later years Durey took control of the company and sold most of the lots. He persuaded the power company to build a new dam controlling the level of the lakes.

5. The slipper company was taken over by Willett, Sears and Company of Boston and later went under the control of Boston banks. It is still a thriving industry. At various times slippers, shoes, parts and ornaments, bats, bowling pins, piano parts and many other articles either made of wood or centering about the shoe and slipper industry have been made in Dolgeville. Four strong presidents of Daniel Green Company have been W. R. Green, James A. Green, Warren Reardon, and John Reardon.

6. *Evening Times* (Little Falls), January 30, 1922.

7. Account by Alva Gardner, taped for the Dolgeville Adult Education Folklore and Local History class.

8. Alfred Dolge's ashes are buried at the highest point of the Dolgeville cemetery, with a monument inscribed "The Founder of Dolgeville." Slightly below it is a monument to Rudolf Dolge, 1869-1950, Anita Heller-Schneller Dolge, 1870-1953, and Alfred Dolge, Jr., 1893-1918. (The latter came back to enlist in World War I and died in the United States.)

9. Rudolf Dolge sent to the Dolgeville Public Library a large collection of papers detailing his work in Venezuela.

10. John C. Freund, "An Inspiring Memorial Tribute to Alfred Dolge," *Music Trades*, February 11, 1922 (pp. 15-19). After leaving Dolgeville, Freund had been editor of *Music Trades* and *Musical America.*

INDEX